All good wishes

from

[signature]

NORTH-EAST HISTORY FROM THE AIR

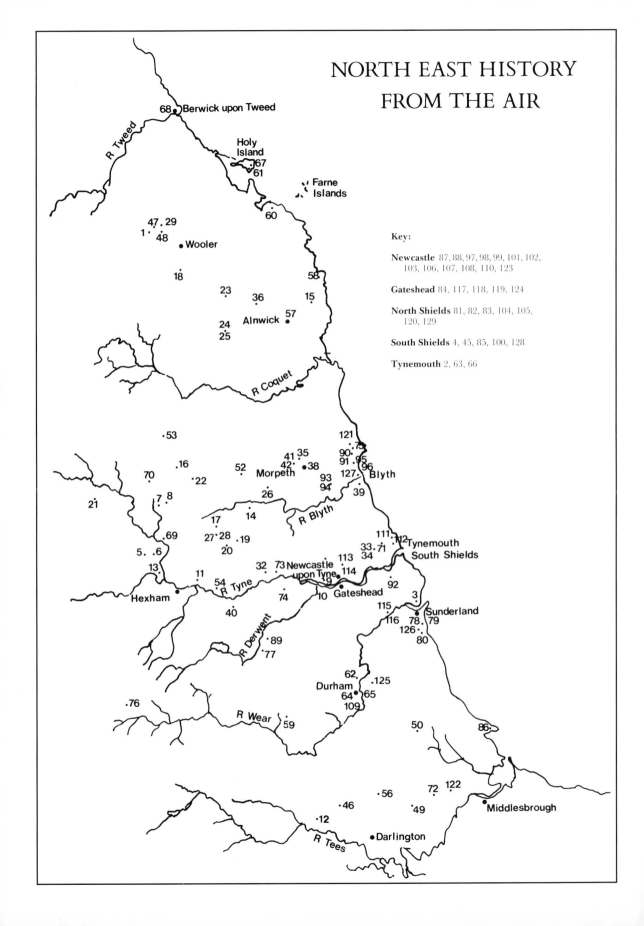

NORTH EAST HISTORY
FROM THE AIR

68 ● Berwick upon Tweed

R Tweed

Holy
Island
67
61

Farne
Islands

60

47 . 29
1 . . 48
● Wooler

18

23
36
15

24
25
Alnwick 57

R Coquet

Key:

Newcastle 87, 88, 97, 98, 99, 101, 102, 103, 106, 107, 108, 110, 123

Gateshead 84, 117, 118, 119, 124

North Shields 81, 82, 83, 104, 105, 120, 129

South Shields 4, 45, 85, 100, 128

Tynemouth 2, 63, 66

● 53

121
90 75
16 91 95
70 52 41 35 96
22 42 38 127 Blyth
Morpeth 93 39
26 94

7 8 14
17
21 27 28 19
69 20
5 . 6 111 12
13 32 73 33 71 Tynemouth
11 Newcastle 113 34 South Shields
54 R Tyne upon Tyne 114
74 9 92
10 Gateshead 3
Hexham 115
40 116 78 79 Sunderland
126
80

R Derwent
89
77

62
Durham .125
64 65
109

76

R Wear 59

50
86

72 122
56
46 49
Middlesbrough
12

R Tees ● Darlington

NORTH-EAST HISTORY FROM THE AIR

Norman McCord

Phillimore

1991

Published by
PHILLIMORE & CO. LTD.
Shopwyke Hall, Chichester, Sussex

ISBN 0 85033 787 9

Printed and bound in Great Britain by
BIDDLES LTD.,
Guildford, Surrey

Introduction

The aerial photographs which form the core of this book were taken by the author
in the course of a lengthy but part-time campaign which covered most of the third
quarter of this century. The cost of the work was met mainly by successive grants
from the Research Fund of the University of Newcastle upon Tyne, with smaller
contributions from the Research Fund of the Society of Antiquaries of Newcastle
upon Tyne and from the author. By far the greater part of the flying was provided by
the training aircraft of the Newcastle and Sunderland Flying Clubs piloted by the
club instructors. The first camera used was an ex-U.S. Air Force K-20 bought by the
university for £20 in the 1950s, and when that venerable instrument was worn out
most of the work was done using the author's own 35mm. cameras. The
photographic processing was provided by the Audio-Visual Centre of the University
of Newcastle upon Tyne, where the staff have been uniformly helpful. Prints of the
photographs themselves are held in the university's Department of Archaeology
where, as one part of a much larger collection of aerial photographs of the region,
they are arranged topographically according to Ordnance Survey map references.
The negatives form part of the university's general photographic collection in its
Audio-Visual Centre. In many cases black and white prints are supplemented by
colour transparencies. Copies of the photographs are also held in the national
collection of the Royal Commission for Historical Monuments (England).

North-East England is taken here to include the old 'Three Counties' of Durham,
Newcastle upon Tyne and Northumberland, together with Berwick and the
Cleveland fringe of North Yorkshire. Summaries of this aerial photography were
published in *Archaeologia Aeliana* in 1968 and 1971.[1] Subsequently a selection of the
photographs was also published in two booklets, one for Northumberland and one
for Durham.[2] Since both of these are not now available, in 1989 the Association of
Northumberland Local History Societies suggested the publication of another
selection from the collection; this initiative has led to the provision of the present
version.

This compilation has a limited objective, the publication of a selection of aerial
photographs from a single source. In the years since the Second World War, aerial
photography has made a significant contribution to our understanding of North-
East history, including the work of other participants such as Professor J. K. St
Joseph, Professor Peter Salway, Professor Dennis Harding, Mr. Tim Gates and
Captain Ray Selkirk. The photographs offered here can therefore give only a partial
indication of the ways in which aerial photography has improved our appreciation
of the region's history. Moreover, the techniques and the exploitation of aerial

photography have become increasingly sophisticated in the years since most of these photographs were taken. This is not to say that it is no longer possible for an amateur archaeologist to make a valuable contribution in this field of activity.

The choice of photographs for inclusion has not been easy, but the selection has been directed to illustrate some of the distinctive features of this particular campaign. From the beginning of the work represented here, it was appreciated that the most economical and useful application of the technique of archaeological aerial photography involved the abandonment of the chronological limitations which had been common in earlier ventures. It was understandable of course that much earlier effort had concentrated upon those early contexts where other forms of historical evidence were either non-existent or seriously defective. However, collieries and shipyards, modern housing, schools and universities are as much a part of the region's evolution as henge monuments, Roman forts and deserted medieval villages. This all-period approach is illustrated here in ways which indicate the breadth of interest which aerial photography can serve. The cost of flying has materially increased in recent years and it makes good sense to profit from the investment in as many ways as possible.

I am grateful to Dr. Constance Fraser for helpful advice which has enabled me to correct some errors in the initial draft. Professor George Jobey has also provided useful advice on some photographs. Mr. Frank Carr kindly drew the map which accompanies the list of sites included here. The comments on some of the Durham photographs owe much to contributors to the *Durham History from the Air* booklet of 1971; this applies to Monkwearmouth and Jarrow (Professor Rosemary Cramp), South Shields, Piercebridge and Garmondsway (Dr. Brian Dobson), Heighington and Carlton (Dr. Brian Roberts), Castle Hill, Bishopton (Miss Barbara Harbottle), Raby Castle (Mrs. June Crosby), Durham City (Michael Drury and Linda Proom), Killhope and Castleside (Dr. Frank Atkinson), St Aidan's College, University of Durham (Irene Hindmarsh), and Carrville Intersection (Mr. W. L. Pattison).

Mr. Hylton Charlton, Dr. Constance Fraser and Professor Philip Yarrow played a prominent part in the discussions which led to the publication of this book, and I am grateful to them. This book is dedicated to the Association of Northumberland Local History Societies and especially to its Secretary, Mrs. Janet Brown, who has done so much for local history in the county.

Notes to Introduction

1. N. McCord and G. Jobey, Notes on air reconnaissance in Northumberland and Durham: I', *Archaeologia Aeliana*, 4th Series, Vol. XLVI (1968), pp. 51-67: Notes on air reconnaissance in Northumberland and Durham: II', *Archaeologia Aeliana*, 4th Series, Vol. XLIX (1971), pp. 119-30.
2. N. McCord (ed.), *Durham History from the Air*, Durham County Local History Society, 1971: N. McCord, *Northumberland History from the Air*, Newcastle, Frank Graham, 1972.

List of Aerial Photographs

'Place' refers to the name by which the site has been entered in the photographic collection held in the Department of Archaeology, University of Newcastle upon Tyne. This is followed by an Ordnance Survey map reference, and by the reference number of the negative held in the University's Audio-Visual Centre. An accompanying sketch map gives an approximate position for the photographs, using the numbering in the list which follows.

Place	O.S. Map Reference	Negative Number
1. East Marleyknowe	NT943324	G/072095/11
2. Tynemouth	NZ374694	G/029455/24
3. Monkwearmouth	NT403577	A/087795/4
4. South Shields	NZ366678	A/090827/65
5. Housesteads	NY790687	A/129382/9
6. Carrawburgh	NY859711	A/050610/31
7. Risingham	NY891863	A/050610/20
8. Fourlaws	NY905825	A/078638/6
9. Washing Well (distant)	NZ219603	A/069486/67
10. Washing Well	NZ219603	A/069599/7
11. Corbridge	NY982647	A/083290/15
12. Piercebridge	NZ210158	A/083494/7
13. Warden Hill	NY904678	A/130038/1
14. Berry Hills	NY967837	A/129323/12
15. Howick Hill Barrow	NU234176	G/030032/24
16. Harehaugh	NY970998	G/017030/25
17. Plashetts	NY965814	G/014294/22
18. North Heddon Moor	NT998219	G/030032/30
19. Colwell	NY946762	G/014294/27
20. Gunner Crag	NY915750	A/075426/3
21. Smalesmouth	NY734855	A/077289/23
22. Manside Cross	NY984921	G/014714/38
23. Brands Hill	NT980245	G/030032/42
24. High Knowes A	NT971125	G/025220/15
25. High Knowes B	NT971125	G/025220/5

26.	Edge House	NZ054806	G/014714/39
27.	Quarry House (distant)	NY965814	G/014294/34
28.	Quarry House	NY965814	G/014294/25
29.	Milfield	NT437337	A/069571/55
30.	West Akeld Steads	NT957307	A/069656/154
31.	Sandy House, Milfield	NT936326	A/069484/29
32.	High Close House West	NZ118658	A/044694/6
33.	Hazlerigg South 1	NZ235716	A/044482/12
34.	Hazlerigg South 2	NZ234715	A/044413/12
35.	Whittle Hill	NZ120858	A/050756/13
36.	West Bewick Bridge	NU047222	A/069656/162
37.	Flodden Edge	NT914349	A/069656/143
38.	Mitford Steads South	NZ173839	G/034485/54
39.	Bebside	NZ277816	A/083676/10
40.	Apperley Dene	NZ056581	A/069083/10
41.	Hartburn West	NZ081867	G/040975/12
42.	Hartburn West (houses)	NZ081867	A/076378/34
43.	Burradon (crop mark)	NZ270730	G/029455/10
44.	Burradon (excavation)	NZ270730	A/062679/28
45.	St Paul's, Jarrow	NZ338653	A/075487/7
46.	Heighington	NZ247223	A/069589/58
47.	Milfield	NT943340	A/079303/1
48.	Thirlings	NT956323	A/076367/40
49.	Carlton	NZ395218	A/074356/21
50.	Garmondsway	NZ342348	A/069890/11
51.	South Middleton	NZ055841	A/129323/9
52.	The Fawns	NZ007853	G/014294/33
53.	Elsdon Castle	NY937036	A/079303/9
54.	Styford Motte	NZ015625	A/057736/7
55.	Warkworth Castle	NU247057	A/073184/19
56.	Castle Hill, Bishopton	NZ367208	A/074356/9
57.	Alnwick Castle	NU187137	A/033546/1
58.	Dunstanburgh Castle	NU257220	A/087795/3
59.	Raby Castle	NZ128217	A/069589/33
60.	Bamburgh Castle	NU184352	A/083676/19
61.	Lindisfarne Priory	NU125417	A/090827/23
62.	Finchale Priory	NZ296472	A/069053/23
63.	Tynemouth Priory	NZ374694	A/073184/8
64.	Durham (distant view)	NZ274420	A/071525/14
65.	Durham Cathedral	NZ274420	A/070630/20
66.	Spanish Battery, Tynemouth	NZ374692	G/029455/20
67.	Lindisfarne Castle	NT136417	A/090827/25
68.	Berwick	NT999528	A/083676/36
69.	Chipchase Castle	NY882758	A/084329/27
70.	Redesdale Iron Works	NY882758	A/050610/22
71.	Seaton Delaval Hall	NZ323766	A/083262/11

72.	Wynyard Park	NZ421257	A/083783/22
73.	Close House	NZ658127	A/044694/11
74.	Gibside	NZ176588	A/068718/9
75.	Woodhorn Farm	NZ297890	A/062679/12
76.	Killhope	NY827429	A/057736/20
77.	Vane Tempest Colliery	NZ425503	A/069656/11
79.	Seaham Harbour	NZ434493	A/069656/14
80.	Seaham Harbour Staiths	NZ434493	A/069083/32
81.	Albert Edward Dock	NZ352688	A/050097/15
82.	Dene Staith	NZ352688	A/050097/18
83.	Whitehill Point	NZ350663	A/050097/30
84.	Derwenthaugh	NZ210630	A/050605/13
85.	Tyne Dock	NZ354650	A/050097/39
86.	West Hartlepool	NZ517333	A/069589/45
87.	Walker Naval Yard	NZ296635	A/083389/10
88.	Swan Hunters, Wallsend	NZ297637	A/090827/10
89.	Consett Iron Works	NZ100505	A/069432/30
90.	Ashington	NZ265878	A/050342/25
91.	Ashington, Hirst End	NZ278875	A/050342/23
92.	Boldon Colliery	NZ344623	A/104440/1
93.	Netherton (distant view)	NZ243826	A/062679/3
94.	Netherton village	NZ243826	A/062679/2
95.	North Seaton	NZ290857	G/051133/13
96.	North Seaton (demolition)	NZ290857	A/083262/13
97.	Newcastle, Ouseburn	NZ264644	A/079303/8
98.	Central Newcastle	NZ252647	A/079303/6
99.	Grainger Market, Newcastle	NZ252647	A/079303/4
100.	South Shields	NZ364677	A/050097/11
101.	Newcastle	NZ236647	A/063350/15
102.	Newcastle	NZ236647	A/050605/11
103.	Newcastle	NZ223634	A/050605/3
104.	North Shields	NZ354677	A/090827/6
105.	North Shields	NZ346689	A/090827/3
106.	Newcastle University	NZ249651	A/079303/5
107.	Castle Leazes Halls	NZ238240	A/063350/15
108.	Newcastle	NZ256641	A/090827/12
109.	St Aidan's College, Durham	NZ267410	A/069053/24
110.	Newcastle Fair, 1972	NZ246665	A/083025/6
111.	Whitley Bay, Spanish City	NZ355726	A/087795/6
112.	Cullercoats	NZ360714	A/062679/32
113.	Killingworth New Town	NZ275715	A/090827/16
114.	Killingworth New Town	NZ275715	A/090827/14
115.	Washington New Town	NZ317578	A/074315/27
116.	Washington New Town	NZ317578	A/074315/6
117.	Gateshead	NZ270602	A/083290/20
118.	Doxford Park, Sunderland	NZ380525	A/083783/3

119.	Team Valley Trading Estate	NZ244602	A/069153/26
120.	North Shields	NZ320685	A/090827/56
121.	Lynemouth, Alcan Smelter	NZ297904	A/083262/16
122.	Billingham, I.C.I.	NZ470220	A/069589/39
123.	Tyne Bridges	NZ254636	A/075279/1
124.	Tyne Bridges	NZ254636	A/075279/5
125.	Carrville Intersection	NZ307447	A/069656/21
126.	Ryhope Pumping Station	NZ407529	A/077289/17
127.	Blyth Power Station	NZ300832	A/090827/46
128.	South Shields, Hospital	NZ366644	A/117872/3
129.	North Shields, Smith's Dock	NZ356676	A/090827/1

Commentary

(The numbers in brackets inserted in the text refer to the photographs as listed above.)

The environment in which we now live is not of our making, nor of the making of our parents' or grandparents' generations, but represents the sum of human activities within the region since the first wandering parties of hunters and food-gatherers penetrated the coastal plain and the river valleys perhaps 10,000 years ago. Our present landscape includes elements accumulated over this long time span, and the first four photographs are intended to illustrate something of this diversity.

At East Marleyknowe (1), just to the south of the village of Milfield in north Northumberland, there is a wealth of varied historical evidence. At bottom left is part of the dispersal areas of the Royal Air Force airfield at Milfield, built shortly before the Second World War and used for a variety of purposes throughout that conflict. Since this photograph was taken, most of the airfield's area has been removed in quarrying for sand and gravel. To the right lies a road, the modern A697, running on the line of an early 19th-century turnpike road. To the right or west of the road lies a field of barley. Within this crop a broken circular feature marks the site of a ditch around a henge, or early religious monument (see also 30), dating from the late Neolithic or early Bronze Age, perhaps 4,000 years ago. It may also be possible to pick out a much slighter circular crop-mark above and to the left of the henge, almost certainly marking a burial of similar antiquity. Just below the henge a dark streak runs through the crop before bending to pass under the road; this represents the insertion of a North Sea gas main.

In the next photograph we look over the north side of the mouth of the Tyne (2). The nearest headland is crowned by the ruins of Tynemouth Priory and Castle (see also 63), but underlying these medieval structures are the remains of native settlements going back into pre-Roman times.[1] On the further headland to the left lies the Spanish Battery (see also 66), a defensive work for the harbour begun in the 16th century but with substantial later modifications. To the right of the Spanish Battery, behind a row of coastguard houses, stands the region's monument to a famous son, Admiral Lord Collingwood, Nelson's second-in-command at Trafalgar. The monument bears a colossal statue of Collingwood and four guns from his flagship. Between the two headlands, at the left of the photographs, a short stretch of the North Pier can be seen. This is a late 19th-century structure which, with its

1. East Marleyknowe: multi-period site.

2. Tynemouth: multi-period site.

3. Monkwearmouth: multi-period site.

4. South Shields: multi-period site.

opposite number to the south, played a crucial role in transforming the Tyne from an unsafe anchorage into a modern harbour. Further up the river, on the right hand bank, it may be possible to make out two white towers. These carry leading lights marking the entry channel into the port before the building of the modern piers and the later lights which they carry.

Near the mouth of the river Wear (3), the time span involved is less extensive, but still striking. Modern shipyards mark the long history of shipbuilding on this river, a story which has only recently come to a sad end, for the time being at least. During their heyday, the Wearside yards notched up some notable success stories, including the development of the Liberty ship during the Second World War and the later SD14 cargo ship, a standardised 14,200 ton cargo vessel designed to replace that famous wartime carrier. Beside the road to the right, a group of modern buildings, incorporating a hexagonal structure, was originally built as a combined trade union office and social club for shipyard workers, becoming a night club in later years. Within the open space — from which high density terrace housing of the later 19th century has been removed in recent years — lies the little church of St Peter's, Monkwearmouth. St Peter's was founded in A.D. 674 at the instance of a Northumbrian nobleman, Benedict Biscop, who persuaded King Ecgfrith to grant royal lands for the endowment of a monastery. This early church is now represented only by the tower and part of the church's west front. With the sister church at Jarrow (see 45), Monkwearmouth has strong associations with the Venerable Bede. Jarrow was a daughter house of Monkwearmouth founded in the 680s, and the two churches were then part of a single organisation.[2]

South Shields (4) presents us with another time sandwich. The large structure at upper centre is the Baring Street Schools, erected in 1883 by the South Shields School Board. That Board had come into existence as a result of the Elementary Education Act of 1870, a landmark in the history of British education. The original schools accommodated 716 children (358 boys, 358 girls) and cost £12,000 to build. They were intended to cater for the children from a rapidly growing area of housing, part of which is represented by the terraces visible in this photograph (see 100 for another view of part of the catchment area of these schools). In a society which as yet gave the preservation of ancient monuments a low priority, the Baring Street Schools, and many terrace houses, were built on top of the Roman fort of South Shields, which had served as the eastern terminus of successive frontier systems. In the early third century, the fort was reconstructed as a major military base supplying the armies of the emperor Septimus Severus during his Scottish campaigns. During the present century, the demolition of some of the Victorian terraces and a prolonged campaign of excavation has facilitated the display of more of the surviving Roman structures, shown in the centre. Since this photograph was taken, the schools have been demolished and the north gate of the Roman fort has been reconstructed in striking fashion on the site of the original gate.

These introductory photographs give some conception of the duration and complexity of the region's evolution. We now turn to illustrate individual phases in the complicated story. The period of the Roman occupation provides a useful starting point. Hadrian's Wall and its associated sites present the most striking

5.   Housesteads: Roman fort on Hadrian's Wall.

6.   Carrawburgh: Roman fort on Hadrian's Wall.

monuments remaining from this period. Housesteads (5) is one of the best known sites in the whole of the Roman Empire. When it was excavated by R. C. Bosanquet in 1898, it produced one of the first complete plans of a Roman fort. Later work, with more sophisticated techniques, has corrected some of those earlier results by separating out different periods of construction more accurately. In this south-facing photograph, the running line of Hadrian's Wall joins the fort's north-east corner at bottom left. Around the playing-card shape of the fort, the fort wall with

7.   Risingham: Roman outpost fort north of Hadrian's Wall.

its gates and towers is clearly visible. Inside, at bottom left, barrack blocks are in process of excavation in this 1979 view. It may be possible to pick out how in later periods the once continuous barrack blocks were reconstructed as lines of separate buildings, perhaps reflecting changes in army organisation in the later Roman period. To the right of the barracks lie the fort's two granaries or storehouses, the upper one altered by the insertion of a later corn-drying kiln. Above the granaries lies the fort's headquarters building, with the camp hospital to the right. Still higher lies the extensive commandant's house, built around a central courtyard. The fort's latrine lies to the right of the tower in the top left corner, with some of the buildings of the civil settlement outside the fort visible nearby.

Housesteads has been extensively excavated on more than one occasion and is a well-known centre of visitors' interest. Other forts on the wall are less well known.

Excavations on the neighbouring wall fort of Carrawburgh (6) in 1967-9 revealed that the remains were much scantier than at Housesteads.[3] No doubt much of the building stone here had provided a useful quarry for later generations of builders. This fort was added to the wall line after the original group of forts was constructed, for the filled-in ditch of the Vallum, an earthwork running behind the wall, lies under the fort. The wall itself runs here on the line of the modern road. In the little valley to the left (west), a temple of Mithras, visible as a small rectangular structure in a cleared enclosure, has been excavated and preserved on site. Mithras, originally an eastern deity, was worshipped by followers in at least three of the forts on Hadrian's Wall, and probably in more.[4] A little distance below this exposed building, another temple, dedicated to the Nymphs, has been excavated but then covered up again. Further up the little valley, towards the road, Coventina's Well, a sacred spring, was discovered to contain thousands of Roman coins when excavated in the 19th century.

Roman influence did not stop with the line of Hadrian's Wall, for the area to the north was subject to surveillance. In the third and fourth centuries a group of outpost forts was occupied to the north of the wall, on both the east and west sides. Risingham (7) is one of these, situated on one of the main Roman routes to the north, Dere Street. Although again much of the masonry was subsequently removed and re-used by later generations, the fort platform still stands out clearly, with its multiple ditches surrounding it. Although some excavations took place here in both the 19th and 20th centuries, Risingham has seen less modern disturbance than wall forts like Housesteads or Chesters, and may well provide future generations with a useful reservoir of archaeological evidence.

Hadrian's Wall provides the best known group of Roman sites in the region, but there are many others. There are numerous examples of Roman temporary camps, relatively slight defensive structures erected as overnight or short term camps, either by a formation on the march or for soldiers engaged in construction or repair work on some road or other installation. Fourlaws (8) is a good example. Within its relatively slight ramparts, carrying a perimeter palisade, the unit involved would have pitched its leather tents in a layout mirroring the allocation of space within a permanent fort; the unit commander's tent would be placed in the same position as the headquarters building within a fort. To the right of the camp the Roman road Dere Street underlies the modern A68 and then ran along the line of the field wall where the modern road veers off to the right. The left hand side of the Roman camp has been interfered with at a later date (the Roman camp adjoins an area which served as a military tank testing ground in recent years), but the other three sides give an idea of the nature of these relatively slight defensive sites. The line of the rampart is clear enough, and at three points it is possible to pick out the way in which a curving line of rampart was continued inside the camp to make control of the vulnerable entrances more certain.

At Housesteads, Carrawburgh, Risingham and Fourlaws, aerial photography provides a useful visual aid rather than anything indispensable to understanding; remains of the stone buildings at Housesteads or the Carrawburgh Mithraeum can be readily seen on the ground and even at Fourlaws it is possible to follow the slight perimeter mound. In other instances aerial photography becomes an essential tool of research. Where centuries of agriculture have removed all surface traces, patterns of early occupation can still be retrieved by observing the behaviour of growing crops, which may respond to differences in soil conditions due to past human activity on the site. From the air such variations in a growing crop can often be distinguished as a meaningful pattern, although a ground observer would not be able to appreciate this form of evidence because of the crucial difference in perspective. These variations within growing crops can take different forms. Undisturbed areas, where the earth has been consolidated over millennia, will have a consistency differing from areas which have been dug into. Where a ditch has been cut through topsoil and subsoil, even if the surface has subsequently been levelled, the filling of the old ditch will reveal differences in character and consistency from undisturbed areas nearby. Where the remains of stone buildings lie a short distance below the surface of the ground, their presence will affect fertility and moisture retention along the old building lines. Crops vary in their capacity for exhibiting such differences. Cereal crops are particularly useful here (see for instance, 1, 9-12, 29-43). A crop of barley growing over filled-in ditches may be stronger than that growing over a hard-packed sand and gravel subsoil. The crop

8. Fourlaws: Roman temporary camp.

along the ditch lines may well be higher than surrounding plants, and carry heavier grain heads which will reflect sunshine more brightly when ripe. A crop growing over different soil conditions will show colour differences representing varying moisture availability and a varying pace of ripening. Crops growing over concealed stone foundations may be discernibly thinner and weaker than those in surrounding areas. For archaeological purposes, it usually matters little what form a differential growth takes, as long as there is some kind of crop marking which reflects past human activity in the area concerned.

In the summer of 1970, such conditions revealed the existence of superimposed Roman forts only a few miles from Newcastle, at Washing Well, west of Gateshead (9 and 10). The first photograph gives a distant view of the site, with the fort marked by an arrow, which indicates the extensive field of view to the north which the position offers. The second photograph gives a close-up of the crop-marks themselves. On some of these photographs it is even possible to pick out small dot-like crop-marks beside entrances, which must represent the pits which held the main uprights for timber gates. This adds to the value of the discovery, for the presence of timber gates indicates a date relatively early during the Roman occupation, a time before the more general adoption of building of forts in stone. Although early Roman frontier dispositions have long been recognised west of Corbridge, the Washing Well discovery presents an opportunity for finding out more about these installations in the eastern sector of the Tyne-Solway gap.

In the next photograph we are looking westward over the Roman site west of the medieval and modern village of Corbridge (11). This is another Roman site which has been much excavated over the years. At present only a small part of the total area occupied during the Roman period is exposed and open to the public, but crop-marks in the field to the west give an indication of the wider area of Roman activity. The principal streets of a settlement which became an important town in late Roman times show clearly, no doubt because the hard-packed road metalling is affecting the growth of the crop. Towards top right a double darker line indicates a perimeter around the area of Roman occupation at one period, with the possible site of a small gate. Away to the south, at Piercebridge on the river Tees (12), similar effects can be seen. The known Roman fort, and the medieval village, lie below the area of the photograph. The crop-marks in the Tofts field to the east of the fort show the street pattern of the little Romanised town which grew up around this fort guarding the river-crossing, and also the fainter outlines of many of the town's rectangular timber buildings.

The Romans are often seen as a people belonging to our remote past, to our ancient history. It is worth reflecting that something like three-quarters of the time span of human presence in this region had already passed when the first Roman soldiers arrived here late in the first century A.D. Behind the three centuries of Roman occupation there lie the long, slow thousands of years of the Mesolithic, Neolithic, Bronze Age and Iron Age periods. In contrast to the long interest in Roman remains, it is only in comparatively recent years that much attention has been paid to the older native settlements of the region. The early native sites lack the rich and varied artifacts, the coins, the inscriptions, the masses of good pottery

9. Washing Well: distant view of Roman forts revealed by crop-marks.

10. Washing Well: crop-marks of superimposed Roman forts.

11. Corbridge: exposed Roman site and crop-marks indicating wider occupation.

12. Piercebridge: crop-marks of civil settlement outside Roman fort.

and the legacy of classical writers which are so helpful in interpreting Roman sites. In recent years, however, more native sites have been meticulously and painstakingly excavated, while aerial photography has made significant contributions to knowledge of early patterns of settlement and farming. It remains the case that our knowledge of these inherently poorer societies cannot match that of the Roman world, but over the past 40 years or so much has been learned. In some cases we can confidently place a native settlement within a comprehensible historical slot. Warden Hill (13), near Hexham, represents such a case. This photograph, taken while winter sunshine slanted across a light snow cover, shows the earthworks around a small pre-Roman Iron Age hill fort, with two substantial ramparts. At its right side, the ramparts are overlain by a much slighter enclosure, representing a small native village inhabited during the Roman period, after the hill fort itself had been abandoned. There are many parallels within the region for this kind of sequence, but there are also hundreds of known earthworks where the history of the site is more mysterious. They are often scattered thickly over the countryside, representing human activity over widely varying periods. At Berry Hills (14), near Kirkwhelpington, another photograph of a snow-covered winter landscape shows at least seven different earthworks within a relatively small stretch of territory. These remains present a great diversity of size and shape. The small circular structure near Howick Hall (15), however, presents no great mystery, for it closely resembles many examples which have been excavated and studied elsewhere. There can be no doubt that this represents an early burial, with the central barrow surrounded at a little distance by a circular enclosure. Similarly, the sequence involved in the Iron Age hill fort at Harehaugh (16) is reasonably clear because the site closely resembles parallels which have been intensively studied elsewhere in this region or in such nearby areas as Roxburghshire. Part of the story is represented by the single line of rampart curving through the middle of the site. This probably reflects a phase in which a smaller hill fort was enclosed by a single rampart and ditch, and this may itself overlie an earlier palisaded enclosure. The remainder of the early circuit has been swallowed up in more extensive and formidable defences of a kind frequently encountered in the late pre-Roman Iron Age.

There are many known earthworks which cannot be so readily accommodated within a clear historical context. A small square site at Plashetts (17) may well have been a native farmstead occupied during the Roman period, but without excavated dating material this cannot be confidently assumed. Similarly, the site at North Heddon Moor, near Ilderton (18), represents a fortified promontory in the Cheviot Hills, which may well have been occupied in more than one period, but its story remains obscure. At Colwell (19), two separate settlements lie close together. The nearer of the two shows round stone houses clearly exposed, representing an old excavation of the site. They may well have been occupied by natives during the Roman period, but such relatively poor settlements rarely produce much in the way of datable artifacts. On Gunner Crag (20), near Barrasford, a very different layout survives on a rocky crag. The site has obviously been a settlement at some point in time, but its history is not known. At Smalesmouth (21), in the North Tyne valley, the site appears to have experienced at least two main structural phases, with the

13. Warden Hill: Iron Age hill fort and Romano-British settlement.

14. Berry Hills: earthworks west of Kirkwhelpington.

15.   Howick Hill Barrow: earthworks of early burial site.

16.   Harehaugh: Iron Age hill fort.

17.   Plashetts: earthworks, probably of native site of Roman period.

18. North Heddon Moor: promontory site in Cheviot Hills.

19. Colwell: earthworks indicating two adjacent native settlements.

20. Gunner Crag: earthworks indicating enclosures and houses on crag near Barrasford.

21. Smalesmouth: earthworks near Bellingham, indicating occupation in at least two periods.

inner earthworks resembling nearby native sites occupied during the Roman period (see 26-7), but the remainder of the site's history is unknown and the substantial outer perimeter may have nothing to do with the smaller inner complex. Even very striking and impressive earthworks may prove difficult to interpret. Small scale excavations at Manside Cross (22), near Elsdon, in 1959-60, disclosed that there had been previous digging within the massive enclosing earthworks and there was little to be found in the way of helpful dating evidence, despite careful excavation stretching over several weeks. Two worn fragments of Roman pottery were the principal finds, apart from refuse from the 'good living of former antiquaries'.[5] At Brands Hill (23), in the Cheviot Hills near Wooler, two very different sites, both with the remains of round stone houses, lie close together, but may well share no other connection. The problems involved in interpreting these sites can be well illustrated by two adjacent settlements at High Knowes near Alnham.[6] High Knowes A (24) was a homestead site. Two large and two small house sites were found within its enclosure; it was not possible to ascertain whether or not they were all occupied at the same time. No small datable objects of any kind were found on this remote upland site, despite a most careful excavation. High Knowes B (25) lies just over 100 yards away. Within this more complex site 16 house positions could be picked out.

22. Manside Cross: earthworks near Elsdon including substantial ditches and ramparts.

23. Brands Hill: two native settlements in Cheviot Hills near Wooler.

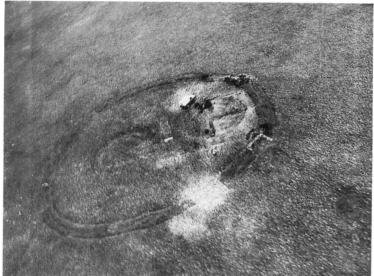

24. High Knowes A: earthwork near Alnham, perhaps Iron Age settlement.

25. High Knowes B: earthworks of early Iron Age and Romano-British native settlement close to previous site.

Here there were a few finds, enough to support a hypothesis that the site was first occupied in early Iron Age times, some time after 700 B.C., and that after a gap in occupation the site was re-used during the Roman period. It is uncertain how far this conclusion could be applied also to the more barren neighbour site.

Despite the problems encountered in dating these early native sites, a great deal of progress has been made in establishing a sequence of settlement types for the Bronze Age, the Iron Age and the native society of the Roman period. A long and patient campaign of field work backed by selective excavation has enabled Professor George Jobey to illuminate much of the evolution of native settlement patterns within the region.[7] One example of this progress has been the identification of a particular form and sequence of native settlements common in the North Tyne valley. Bradford Edge House (26) provides an example of a kind of native farming homestead occupied during the Roman period. The site is surrounded by a rampart and ditch of no great strength. The entrance is on the right (east) in this photograph. From the entrance a raised causeway runs to another raised area across the settlement. Traces of round stone houses can be seen to the rear of the enclosure. Quarry House (27-8) is an even clearer example, though it is uncertain whether or not the outer ditch and mound here belong to the Romano-British farmstead phase. The light patch showing on the first photograph represents an early and unsophisticated excavation of one of the round stone houses. The combination of field work with selective excavation has produced in the North Tyne valley a clear demonstration of a sequence of native farmstead types, developing from an early Iron Age form with wooden huts inside a palisaded enclosure, to stone-built settlements with round stone houses, including Edge House and Quarry House, occupied during the Roman period. A series of excavations has shown that the later stone settlements commonly overlie timber predecessors. Of course, even the roughly built stone native houses of the second century A.D. are primitive compared with contemporary building techniques in the Roman sites themselves.

As with the Roman sites, the study of the early native cultures has been affected by differences in the preservation of surface remains. The last few examples (13-28) all lie in hilly and relatively infertile ground. If a distribution map of known early native sites had been studied at the end of the Second World War, one anomaly would immediately have leaped to the eye. While there were scores, even hundreds, of settlements of varying size and shape in the hills and moors, there were scarcely any to be seen in the fertile coastal plain and river valleys. This apparent imbalance was always suspect, and in more recent years intensive aerial survey has done much to correct it. Even where centuries of cultivation have destroyed all surface traces of ancient settlement, crop-marks continue to present the aerial observer with signs of human activity which may be 2,000 years old or more. Even where there has been intensive aerial survey over a number of years, variations in weather conditions and crop distribution continue to bring new evidence to light each year.

Sometimes one field can reveal many traces of human activity. Just to the east of a group of council houses at the south end of the village of Milfield (29), correlation of a series of photographs shows that at one time or another there have been at least eight different sites in this single field. Even in this single photograph, several crop-

26. Bradford Edge House: earthworks of Romano-British native settlement, perhaps overlying Iron Age homestead.

27. Quarry House: earthworks of Romano-British native settlement, perhaps overlying Iron Age homestead.

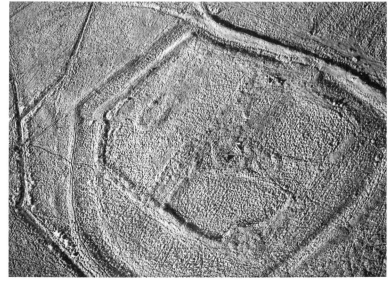

28. Quarry House: closer view.

29.   Milfield: miscellaneous crop-marks to south of Milfield village.

30.   West Akeld Steads: crop-mark of late Neolithic or early Bronze Age henge monument near Wooler.

marks indicate ditches around a variety of sites. As with earthwork sites like Warden Hill (13), Howick Hill (15) or Harehaugh (16), some of the crop-mark sites so closely resemble examples studied and dated elsewhere that they can be readily fitted into a historical slot. At West Akeld Steads, near Wooler (30), a large oval site is recognisably a henge, a religious monument of a well known type (an example of a different but equally well established type of henge appears in 1). Broad arcs of ditch surround an area in which large pits are represented by small individual crop-marks, with a smaller group in the centre. These pits probably held uprights, forming a kind of miniature Stonehenge of the late Neolithic or Early Bronze Age. In the field to the left, at least one of the smaller crop-marks probably represents a prehistoric burial. The henge here is one of a substantial group of such monuments found in this area of north Northumberland, the Milfield plain, which must have held a substantial and organised population about 4,000 years ago.

Many of the region's crop-marks, like its earthworks, remain more mysterious. At Sandy House (31), near the village of Milfield, parallel crop-marks indicate part of the line of a series of 'avenues' which have been found in this area. Their purpose and significance is unknown, but they often run close to or even through henge monuments. Two circular crop-marks may well be early burial sites. What may be the corner of a rectangular site peeps out from the line of trees and its ditch seems to over-ride the avenue. Often a crop-mark discovery offers little more than a simple enclosure. At High Close House West (32), a rectangular ditch with an eastern entrance (indicated by a gap in the perimeter ditch) has only vague suggestions of other features, though the darker patches within the ditch may represent house sites. Sometimes we are given more. At Hazlerigg South 1 (33) there is a rectangular site apparently surrounded by two ditches, with some indications of round houses inside. Within the same field Hazlerigg South 2 (34) is a crop-mark of different character, probably with an eastern entrance (to the left). Whether these two sites share any connection other than proximity is unknown. Many of the crop-mark discoveries have not yet been tied down in time. The double enclosure on Whittle Hill (35), a few miles west of Morpeth, may owe its shape simply to the topographical factor of being built on a round hill.

Sometimes the crop-marks are more revealing. At West Bewick Bridge (36), south of Wooler, a roughly rectangular site with a western entrance is flanked to the right by three circular crop-marks, which may well be burials. At Flodden Edge (37), near Milfield, two roughly rectangular ditches enclosed a central area which held a series of round houses. There is an entrance in the eastern side, and a much slighter enclosure seems to be attached to the same side. From some angles, it would be possible to mistake this site for a regular Roman military fortlet (a mistake which has been made in the past in similar contexts, see 40-2), though from other angles, as here, the photographs make it clear that the shape is less regular and more native-looking than that. The indications of round houses inside also suggest a native rather than a Roman context. In view of the clarity of the principal features here, it is worth emphasising that these features represent variations in the behaviour of a growing crop; there is nothing to see here when the field is ploughed, no distinctive features until the crop begins to develop.

Crop-marks cannot be relied upon to show every year. Mitford Steads South (38) is a site of potential interest in relation to native farmsteads occupied during the Roman period (see also 39, 43-4). It appears to consist of a roughly rectangular inner enclosure, with an east-facing entrance and one large central round house. A more widely spaced outer enclosure surrounds the homestead, and the area between the two enclosing ditches seems to be divided, perhaps to serve specific farming functions. These details appeared in only one season; although the site was subsequently checked over several years only very faint indications of any crop-marks could be detected on the site. In South-East Northumberland there are a number of examples of sites with two similarly widely spaced rectangular ditches. At Bebside (39), near Blyth, a good example lies above the modern road running across the centre of the photograph. The smaller circular feature at bottom right could well represent an early burial, but since the area has seen a great variety of human activity over many centuries this crop-mark may be derived from something very different.

In discussing Flodden Edge (37), it was noted that such a native settlement could, from some angles, be mistaken for a Roman fortlet. This is a point worth further exploration, because it reveals limitations in what aerial photography in isolation may tell us. Such an error, understandable in face of the apparent symmetry of the enclosing ditches and the proximity of the site to a known Roman road, accounted for the long-standing identification of the site at Apperley Dene (40) as a Roman military fortlet. The identification was given at least some support from rather inconclusive excavations in the early 1950s; the arguments in that report were in part derived from early aerial photographs and the site's position by a known Roman road. An accumulation of later aerial photographs, followed by excavation in 1974-5, demonstrated that the site was a native rather than a Roman site.[8] The later excavations were inspired by developments elsewhere in the region. Acceptance of Apperley Dene as a Roman fortlet was partly responsible for a similar identification of crop-marks west of Hartburn (41), close to another known Roman road, the Devil's Causeway. When another similar site was subsequently discovered from the air near Mitford, west of Morpeth, it was suggested that this should be taken as evidence for the existence of a hitherto unknown Roman road running east from the Devil's Causeway, with the Mitford site as a fortlet on it. As more crop-mark sites exhibiting similar characteristics were discovered in various parts of Northumberland, and new photographs taken from different angles suggested that the Mitford and Hartburn sites were less regular in form than first thought, doubts about the Roman nature of these sites grew. Professor Jobey's excavations on the fortlet' at Hartburn in 1971 clinched the matter. Inside the area of the supposed fortlet (42), the characteristic round native houses were found, with clear evidence of frequent re-building indicating a long life as a Romano-British native settlement rather than a Roman military post. The Hartburn demonstration led to the re-interpretation of both the Mitford and Apperley Dene sites. The story provides something of a cautionary tale, indicating that it can be dangerous to place too great a reliance on the evidence of aerial photography alone. The combination of

31. Sandy House, Milfield: miscellaneous crop-marks.

32. High Close House: crop-mark revealing rectangular site near river Tyne.

33. Hazlerigg South 1: crop-mark revealing double-ditched rectangular site with round houses.

34. Hazlerigg South 2: crop-mark of single-ditched site close to previous site.

35. (*left*) Whittle Hill: crop-mark of round double-ditched site on round hill west of Morpeth.

36. (*above*) West Bewick Bridge: crop-mark of possible settlement and burials south of Wooler.

37. (*right*) Flodden Edge: crop-mark of double-ditched rectangular site with round houses near Milfield.

38. Mitford Steads South: crop-marks of site with two widely-spaced ditches west of Morpeth.

39. Bebside: crop-marks of site with two widely-spaced ditches near Blyth.

40. Apperley Dene: crop-mark of native settlement near Roman road, formerly mistakenly identified as Roman fortlet.

aerial photography with selective excavation is a much more potent procedure, as the next two photographs demonstrate.

If, on occasion, aerial photographs could be misinterpreted, the numerous discoveries of crop-mark sites represent a major contribution to our understanding of the region's history. Literally hundreds of these discoveries have taken place since the Second World War, markedly improving the picture of early settlement patterns. Aerial photographs alone cannot, however, provide adequate basis for dating sites and placing them within an intelligible historical sequence. Even where a crop-mark site can be immediately placed within a historical context, this must depend upon the existence of independent dating evidence from parallels elsewhere (as for instance in the case of the henge monuments in 1 and 30). Many of the crop-marks can, however, be grouped into recognisable categories derived from their size and shape. If selective excavation can provide dating evidence for an example of such a type, then that dating can reasonably be extended from the single example to the parallels within the same category. A good example here consists of a group of similar sites to be found at many points in the coastal plain. A rectangular ditched enclosure, with an easterly entrance, contains one large round house. Sometimes there is also an outer enclosure (38 and 39 are possible parallels here). The category is sufficiently distinctive for the dating of one example to be transferred to others. Burradon (43, 44) a few miles north of Newcastle, offers a good instance of the technique.[9] The original aerial photographs show a rectangular site, with an eastern (above in the first photograph) entrance. A variety of crop-mark evidence is exemplified in this photograph. Part of the cereal crop, growing more strongly and higher in a narrow line along a filled-in ditch, has been knocked down by storm damage. Inside, a single large circular house is outlined in another crop-mark. Outside the most obvious ditch, fainter traces, in storm damage at top centre and as a darker line to the left of the photograph, suggest that there may have been an outer enclosure at some distance. Other photographs taken at different times have shown that this was the case. Another photograph (44) shows the site as excavated. The entrance, to the left here, is indicated by the two stub ends of the ditch and slots for gates. The inner circular crop-mark was made by a drainage ditch, part filled with water here, originally dug into the boulder clay around the large central house. This building depended on twin rings of wooden posts, set in the concentric rings of postholes visible. Careful excavation showed that the site had a long life; the remains of smaller, less sophisticated, wooden houses, demonstrably earlier than the large central house, went back to a pre-Roman Iron Age and even a Bronze Age context. The large central house was identified as a native farmstead inhabited during the Roman occupation. This dating can be reasonably extended also to the close parallels already identified elsewhere in the coastal plain of the region. In this way the combination of aerial reconnaissance with selective and careful excavation can make for enhanced understanding of earlier patterns of settlement. In the last 40 years or so, understanding of the early history of the region has become much fuller and more sophisticated. Discoveries from the air, revealing new evidence from earthworks, crop-marks and old agricultural markings, have provided an indispensable contribution to this progress.

41. Hartburn West: crop-mark of native settlement near Roman road, formerly mistakenly identified as Roman fortlet.

42. Hartburn West: native round houses inside settlement during excavation.

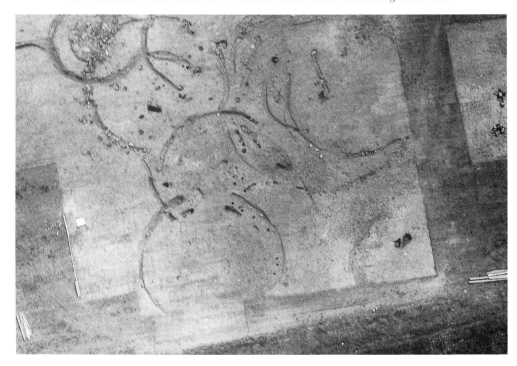

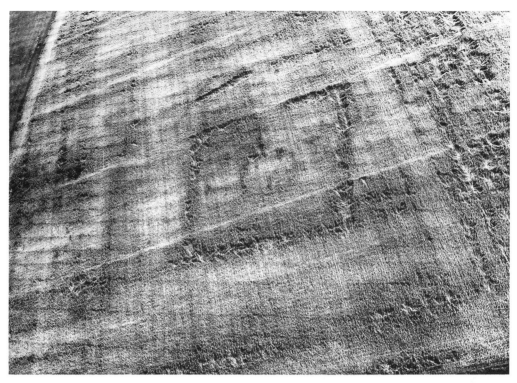

43. Burradon: crop-mark revealing native homestead and enclosing ditches.

44. Burradon: native homestead under excavation.

With the end of the Roman occupation, we lose the thin trickle of datable objects of Roman origin which helped to identify the native sites occupied during the Roman period. There is nothing to suggest that the existing native population disappeared, or even that it soon ceased to occupy the settlements used in the late Roman period. It may be that some of the pre-Roman hill forts were now re-

45. St Paul's, Jarrow: church of Anglo-Saxon foundation.

occupied, but the evidence is too weak to give convincing backing to such a hypothesis. Our knowledge does not begin to broaden out again until the Anglo-Saxon domination of the North East is well established. Before then we have only a few glimmers of light in what remains very much a Dark Age. The archaeological record picks up again in the Anglo-Saxon period, though there are still many gaps.

For many years it has been appreciated that some of the churches of the region contain elements of pre-Conquest architecture, ranging from the almost complete gem at Escomb, near Bishop Auckland, to the fragmentary remains in some of the Tyne valley churches. Two of the older churches derive added interest from their association with the monastery in which Bede spent most of his life. St Peter's, Monkwearmouth, has already been mentioned (3 and note 1). St Paul's, Jarrow (45) still contains the inscription recording its dedication in A.D. 685.

The chancel (to the right in this photograph) formed the nave of a pre-Conquest church, and the tower stands on the site of the porch of that church. We know that the Anglo-Saxon monastery here was burnt by the Danes in 794 and again in 866; any subsequent recovery may have been lost in the 'Harrying of the North' by William I in 1069-70. The existing tower seems to have been part of the reconstruction of the monastery by Abbot Aldwine in the years around 1075.[10] Until 1786 an early nave, of Saxon origin, stood to the left of the tower, but it was then destroyed. In 1866 a new west end of the church, including nave and aisle, was designed by Sir Giles Gilbert Scott. The standing masonry outside the church is a mixture of stray survivals of the medieval monastery and a school and other structures of the 19th century. Since the Second World War excavations directed by Professor Rosemary Cramp have uncovered traces of the Anglo-Saxon monastery under the largely buried remains of its medieval successor.

Although the punitive campaigns carried out by William I in the aftermath of the Northumbrian rebellion in 1069 caused widespread damage, some of the elements

46. Heighington: centre of pre-Conquest 'shire', surviving as important medieval village.

in pre-Conquest Northumbria survived into the Norman world. The church had played a major role in the preservation and development of literacy and culture. Some of the medieval communities preserved some indications of pre-Conquest organisation within the region. As early as the seventh century, the area of the future County Durham seems to have been composed of a series of substantial territorial units, or shires. The headquarters of these units, no doubt also the sites of important churches, usually survived as important villages in the medieval settlement pattern. Staindrop, Gainford, Sockburn and Heighington are examples within the modern county of Durham; in Northumberland, Bedlington and Holy Island provided similar local centres. Heighington (46), in pre-Conquest times the

centre of Heighington-shire, provides a good illustration. The central green, with
the church, a pre-Conquest foundation, is much larger than that of most Durham
villages, and was surrounded by four rows of houses, most contemporary Durham
villages having only two parallel rows (see 49). *Boldon Book*, a survey of the Bishop of
Durham's estates in 1183, preserves a recollection of pre-Conquest organisation
when it refers collectively to the revenue from the mills of Heighingtonshire.
Staindrop is another example of the survival into the Norman era of an established
pre-Conquest local administrative centre, though here the layout consisted
essentially of two long parallel rows of houses, with the church at the east end of the
more northerly row.

It was not until after 1945 that aerial photography made any significant
contribution to our knowledge of the Anglo-Saxon period. In the second book of
his *Ecclesiastical History*, finished about A.D. 731, Bede wrote

> On one occasion when Paulinus came with the king and queen to the royal palace which is
> called Ad Gefrin, he stayed with them there for 36 days ... This residence was abandoned in the
> time of succeeding kings and another palace was built instead at the place called Maelmin.

It was for long uncertain whether or not this account could be taken as a realistic
record. Then Professor J. K. St Joseph discovered, first at Yeavering and then at
Milfield, crop-marks representing these successive royal centres. Yeavering — Bede's
Ad Gefrin — has been excavated, and the extensive report by Dr. Brian Hope Taylor
goes far to confirm the reliability of Bede's reporting of events at the Northumbrian
court in the period of the conversion to Christianity.[11] Milfield (47) — Bede's
Maelmin — has not been excavated, and lies in rougher ground, but is basically
similar to Yeavering. The core of both is a series of rectangular timber halls, which
can be seen within an enclosure in the centre of the photograph of Milfield; this is a
black and white print taken from an original infra-red negative.

One of the problems still facing the historian of Anglo-Saxon Northumbria is the
scale of new settlement involved. Was the Northumbrian kingdom the creation of a
relatively small immigration of rulers, dominating an existing population perhaps of
Romano-British ancestry, or was there a large scale movement of new people into
the area? The answer is still uncertain. The royal centres at both Yeavering and
Milfield were accompanied by a scattering of other buildings which suggests a wider
area of settlement at these key points. A few miles south of Milfield, at Thirlings
(48), a group of rectangular timber buildings resembling some of those in the
palace complex has been excavated and shown to be of Anglo-Saxon date, though
the evidence was not extensive and the site is complicated by the existence there of
a much earlier Neolithic settlement. More recently, additional work based on aerial
photographs has demonstrated the existence of a form of small Anglo-Saxon house
elsewhere in the Northumberland countryside.[12] Anglo-Saxon Northumbria did not
die under the severe Viking attacks, but endured a prolonged period of internal
conflicts and external dangers during the 10th and early 11th centuries, before
becoming at least nominally a part of the emerging Kingdom of the English under
the House of Wessex. Its northern frontier remained uncertain, and indeed the
present border with Scotland is largely a medieval creation.[13] The 'Harrying of the

47. Milfield: crop-mark revealing Anglo-Saxon royal settlement.

48. Thirlings: crop-mark revealing Anglo-Saxon rectangular buildings south of previous site.

North' in 1069-70 has already been mentioned, and seems to have introduced some changes into the settlement pattern. Dr. Brian Roberts has argued that in the aftermath of the northern rebellion and its suppression, new settlements were established within the devastated areas. Villages were planted at more or less regular intervals; within them land-holdings were measured out in symmetrical units of eights and sixteens. The evidence for this planned re-settlement is strongest on the estates of the great ecclesiastical proprietors, such as the Bishop of Durham and the Prior and Convent of Durham, who played such an important role in the region in medieval times. Carlton (49), near Stockton, is a good example, with its parallel rows of houses facing each other across a long narrow green. Behind the houses lie their gardens, stretching to the boundaries of the medieval open fields surrounding the village. Although individual buildings have been built and re-built many times, the basic layout of the village preserves a shape which probably dates to the reign of William the Conqueror.

Not all medieval settlements have survived into modern times, and in both Durham and Northumberland there are good examples of deserted medieval villages. A few miles south of Durham city, Garmondsway (50) is now represented by a single farm. In the *Boldon Book* of 1183 Garmondsway was a prosperous little community, furnishing the Bishop of Durham with an annual rent of 16 hens, 100 eggs and 16 shillings and 8 pence. The village subsequently became part of the endowments of Sherburn Hospital. The date when it ceased to exist as a village is unknown, and a single modern farm bearing the old village name now occupies the site. In this photograph a row of cottages with gardens stretching away to the right can easily be picked out in the alternations of shadow and highlights as slanting sunlight hits the slight earthworks remaining. It is possible that we are only seeing half of the old village. Another similar line of cottages and gardens may have lain to the left across a narrow green, to give a layout like that of Carlton (49); faint traces suggest that this may be the case, with only half of the village affected by ploughing and stone clearance. An even more striking Northumberland example of a deserted medieval village is South Middleton (51), two miles east of Wallington Hall. This is a typical example of a northern stone-built medieval village surrounded by its extensive open fields heavily marked with ridge and furrow cultivation lines. The road, which cuts through the village remains, from top left to centre right in the photograph, was built in the 18th century, by which time the village, which like Garmondsway had known modest prosperity in the 13th century, had largely ceased to exist as a settlement. This photograph is taken with slanting winter sunshine combining with a light snow coverage to emphasise the surviving earthworks of the village and its open fields.

There are some striking variations in the region's medieval settlements. One of the most impressive of these is the Northumberland example at The Fawns (52), near Kirkwhelpington. Substantial ditches and banks enclose an area which contains platforms on which at least three large buildings once stood. Again there are traces of medieval ridge and furrow cultivation markings near the site, some of them overlain by modern field boundaries. There are documentary mentions of occupation here in the 14th, 15th and 16th centuries, but we know little of its functions or its history.

49. Carlton: modern village retaining much of probable 11th-century layout.

50. Garmondsway: earthworks of deserted medieval village south-east of Durham.

51. South Middleton: earthworks of deserted medieval village near Belsay.

52. The Fawns: earthworks of
unusual medieval settlement west of
Kirkwhelpington.

53. Elsdon Castle: earthworks of early
medieval motte and bailey castle,
probably of early 12th century.

54. Styford Motte: earthwork of motte,
only visible vestige of early medieval
castle near river Tyne.

The history of the region during the medieval centuries was profoundly affected by the nature of Anglo-Scottish relations and the state of the border. The region's status as a frontier zone has left its mark on the archaeological record in a fine series of castles. Elsdon Castle (53), if not at first sight particularly prepossessing, is one of the most remarkable of these. Its interest lies primarily in its character as a fine example of an early Norman castle. It was built to serve as the centre of the new barony of Redesdale, held by the Umfraville family, perhaps as late as the reign of Henry I. Elsdon's occupation was short-lived, for it was soon displaced as the Umfraville seat by Harbottle Castle. Harbottle underwent subsequent remodellings and re-buildings in stone, but Elsdon was abandoned and remains the best example within the region of an early motte and bailey castle. The two main elements — the motte, or fortified mound, and the bailey, or fortified courtyard — are clearly visible. We must imagine the motte crowned with a timber palisade around its perimeter, and probably a wooden tower inside, while another palisade would stand on the rampart around the bailey, protecting the hall, chapel, stables, kitchen and similar buildings. In some cases, the surviving traces of early medieval fortifications are even slighter. At Styford (54), in the Tyne valley, only the rounded motte remains of an early castle there. In other cases, the northern castles have complex histories. At Warkworth (55), the sophisticated later castle lies on top of an earlier and simpler castle like that at Elsdon. Here re-building in stone probably dates from the mid-12th century, though most of the extant work is later. The keep, dominating the site and beautifully proportioned, dates from the 14th century and provided its residents with a distinctly higher degree of comfort than the earlier and grimmer keeps of castles like Newcastle or Bamburgh. The Warkworth keep is already almost a combination of castle and late medieval stately home.

In Durham, Castle Hill, Bishopton (56), provides the best example of an early motte and bailey castle in the county. It is recorded in the 1140s and may well have come into existence during the conflicts which marked the reign of Stephen. The greater complexity in comparison with the slightly earlier Elsdon (53) illustrates how the design of castles rapidly became more sophisticated during the medieval period. Alnwick Castle (57), like Warkworth, stands on an earlier motte and bailey construction, but possesses a more complex history. Alnwick first came into Percy hands in 1309 and, with occasional intervals, has been a Percy seat ever since. At top right in this photograph the stables and riding school have been built out through the walls. The approach to the main gate, with the fine enclosed passage or barbican (see 63 for another example) dates from the 14th century. Much of the keep is of the same date, but this central structure was heavily reconstructed in the 18th century and again in the 19th. The curtain wall and its towers also represents a mixed structure, some genuinely medieval, some modern reconstruction. In the third quarter of the 19th century, the Duke of Northumberland could afford, without undue strain, to spend a quarter of a million pounds on refurbishing the castle, an illuminating example of how economic change did not necessarily lead to the displacement of older elements of authority and wealth within the region's society.

Dunstanburgh (58) is a large castle of unusual design.[14] Here the main gatehouse and keep are combined in one strong structure. The castle is essentially an early 14th-century design, and bears some resemblance to the Edwardian castles in Wales, notably Harlech. It was originally built for Thomas, Earl of Lancaster, and reverted to the crown after the earl's downfall in 1322. In 1327 the castle was returned to Thomas' heir, but when Henry IV became king in 1399 the duchy of Lancaster's lands again became crown property. Only relatively slight fortifications were necessary where the castle overlooked the vertical cliffs, but on the more vulnerable south and west the defences were substantial. Raby Castle (59) is one of the most impressive Durham fortresses. In the later medieval period it was for long a stronghold of the Nevilles, but that connection was broken with Charles Neville's participation in the Northern Rising of 1568, which led to Raby's seizure by the crown. In the 1620s Raby and the important nearby village of Staindrop were obtained by the Vane family, who from 1698 held a peerage as Lords Barnard, a title still retained, although the later dignities of Earl of Darlington and Duke of Cleveland have been long extinct. The castle was drastically altered in the mid-19th century under the architect William Burn. During the 18th century the old village of Raby had already been removed to make way for an appropriate park for the castle, with a new village built to house the displaced villagers. The main features of the 14th-century castle survive, with the principal buildings grouped around an inner courtyard. The broad ditch also survives, with a part of it still holding water.

Of all the castles of Northumbria, Bamburgh (60) is the most spectacular. It crowns an impressive basalt crag, starker than the companion crag which provides the site for Dunstanburgh Castle to the south. At Bamburgh the crag rises to 150 feet and provides a long thin north-south platform which was used as a fortress or refuge from very early times. There are prehistoric remains from the site, and Bamburgh was a major centre in Anglo-Saxon times. The keep and some other parts of the castle are basically of 12th-century date. After a long period of decay and relative obscurity, Bamburgh was bought by the engineering and armaments magnate Lord Armstrong in 1890. He carried out major restorations, which greatly impressed contemporaries. Later critics have sometimes been less kind: Professor Pevsner described them as 'grand in scale but wanting in architectural merit', while a more acid judgement has the work combining the 'acme of expenditure with a nadir of intelligent achievement'. The combination of site and structure remains one of the most impressive of the region's monuments.

The north-eastern counties do not possess romantic ruins of medieval monasteries on the same scale as those of Yorkshire or the Scottish border counties, but those which exist are not negligible. Lindisfarne, or Holy Island (61), is among the most interesting, because of its connections with early Christianity in the north. St Aidan came to this island with his band of Irish monks in A.D. 635, at the invitation of the Northumbrian king Oswald. The island's greatest fame arose from its connection with St Cuthbert, whose cult became popular over a wide area. Cuthbert was born in the Lammermuir hills at about the same time as Aidan founded the Lindisfarne community of monks. He entered the monastery at Melrose in 651, the year of Aidan's death, and soon moved to Lindisfarne. Monastic

55. Warkworth Castle: late medieval
stone castle on site of early medieval
motte and bailey castle.

56. Castle Hill, Bishopton:
earthworks of best-preserved early
castle in County Durham.

57. Alnwick Castle: medieval castle,
much altered by successive modern
reconstruction.

58. Dunstanburgh Castle: ruins of medieval castle on basalt crag on Northumberland coast.

59. Raby Castle: medieval castle with substantial 19th-century alterations.

60. Bamburgh Castle: medieval castle, with substantial modern alterations, on basalt crag on Northumberland coast. Important centre at several different periods.

61.   Lindisfarne Priory: ruins of monastery associated with St Cuthbert.

life there proving insufficiently austere, for nine years he lived in a little cell on the smaller Farne Island, until in 685 he reluctantly yielded to the persuasion of King Ecgfrith — the patron of Monkwearmouth and Jarrow — and became bishop at Lindisfarne. Cuthbert died there on 20 March 687, and his fame was such that the monastery rapidly became a place of pilgrimage, with many famous miracles attributed to the saint's intercession. The treasures which accumulated made Lindisfarne an obvious target for Viking raids, and in 875 the monks left the island, carrying with them the relics of St Cuthbert and St Aidan, the head of the Northumbrian king/hero/saint Oswald, and other possessions which included the precious Lindisfarne Gospels, perhaps the finest example of the art of the Golden Age of Northumbria. In 883 they settled at Chester-le-Street, before finally fixing the shrine of St Cuthbert, with all that it meant to the north, on the magnificent promontory site at Durham in 995. The fame of Lindisfarne did not entirely die with the great departure of 875; the pre-Conquest monastery was replaced in the years from 1093 by a monastery of some note. Although the community was usually small, perhaps a dozen monks under a prior, the buildings were stately, and the sanctity of the island still widely recognised. A village or small town grew up around

the priory, while as early as 1344 the monastic community itself had begun to trade
in limestone quarried on the island. After the dissolution of the priory in 1537,
some of its buildings were dismantled to provide stone for the building of Holy
Island Castle (67); despite this and later depredations, the priory ruins still remain
as an attractive monument. In this photograph we are looking north over the priory

62. Finchale Priory: monastic ruins a few miles from Durham.

site to part of the little town; to the left of the ruins lies the parish church of St
Mary, established to serve the growing community beyond the monastery's walls.
Within the priory ruins, the nearest enclosure is the outer court, which contained
the guest house; beyond lie the cloisters with the community's own accommodation
grouped around them. Then at the far end are the ruins of the priory church,
mainly of the 11th and 12th centuries.

The ruins of Finchale Priory (62) nestle in a loop of the river Wear a few miles
from Durham. Its founder was St Godric, whose varied career had included periods
as a pedlar and as a shipowner. He had travelled over much of Europe before
settling at Finchale about 1110. His reputation for sanctity grew, visitors were
attracted to his retreat and a small stone church was built. Godric himself died in
1170, reputedly at the age of 105, and was buried in this early church. The

monastery here was originally founded as a house of Augustinian canons, but by the end of the 12th century Finchale had become a dependent house of the great Benedictine community at Durham, occupied by a few Durham monks under a prior. Fragmentary remains of the earlier monastic structures can be seen in this photograph to the right of the principal ruins. The fine priory church of the 13th century stands out clearly in its cruciform plan, with the cloisters and monastic buildings around them. In the 14th century there were further changes; the church was reduced in size by the removal of its aisles. The main function of the reduced priory in the 14th, 15th and early 16th centuries seems to have been as a place of rest and recuperation for monks from the Durham cathedral community. The accommodation mainly used then is represented by the range of buildings at bottom right of the central group. The priory was dissolved in 1538.

Tynemouth Priory (63) is another monastic site with a long history. On the headland now crowned by the ruins of the priory and castle (see also 2), long

63. Tynemouth Priory: ruins of monastery and castle on headland at mouth of Tyne.

before the Christian church reached the region, a native settlement existed at least as far back as the early Iron Age.[15] The headland was still occupied by a native community in Roman times and held a monastic community in pre-Conquest days; as at Lindisfarne, a medieval monastery was constructed here in the years around 1090. Very little of this Norman church is now visible, but one notable feature is its east end with curving projections for side chapels, now seen in outline within the ruins of the larger church of about 1200 which replaced it. Above the nave of this later church, the cloisters and some of the associated monastic buildings can be picked out. Nothing survives of defences on the headland earlier than the end of the 13th century, and, of the later fortifications, the gatehouse is the principal survivor, seen here at centre right. Like that at Alnwick (57), the gate itself is approached through an enclosed passage or barbican; this must date from the 14th century and may be an imitation of the Alnwick work. Since the priory was dissolved in 1539, the fine headland site at Tynemouth has been used for a variety of military installations, including barracks which survived until the mid-20th century. Little evidence of this long occupation in modern times survives now to distract visitors from the fine medieval ruins by reminding them that the site has been used by man over a very long period.

Durham (64, 65) remains as the most impressive monastic site in the region, and indeed in its majestic combination of structure and setting has been recognised as one of the finest medieval monuments of Western Europe. The first photograph gives an impression of the central site, as the river Wear makes an enormous loop around a narrow and steep promontory. Oddly enough, there is no evidence of substantial occupation here before the establishment of the shrine of St Cuthbert in the last years of the 10th century. With the coming of the Normans, the construction of a castle to guard the narrow neck of land was already under way in the 1070s, while the cathedral itself was begun by Bishop William of St Calais in 1093. In the second photograph there is a closer look at the cathedral, with the cloisters and domestic buildings of its Benedictine community. Beyond it on its mound is the shell keep of the castle, heavily modified in the 19th century. The cult of St Cuthbert made Durham a centre of pilgrimage, especially in March and September, while in addition the town grew as the administrative capital of a prince-bishop who exercised regalian rights throughout the extensive Patrimony of St Cuthbert. This area included not only county Durham but also sizeable outlying territories around Bedlington, Lindisfarne and the mainland opposite, and a third northern shire' around the bishop's border fortress at Norham on Tweed. Of all of the region's inheritance from the medieval centuries, the peninsular core of Durham is the greatest single element. On the peninsular site much of the layout of buildings still reflects a medieval pattern of landholding, with narrow frontages and long rear extensions.

Border warfare did not end with what is commonly seen as the close of the medieval period, and Tudor monarchs expended much effort and money on the defence of England's northern frontier. By this time the hold of the central government on this remote area was already becoming stronger.[16] The principal fortifications remaining from the 16th century are not the work of any baronial

64. Durham City: distant view of promontory site.

65. Durham City: closer view of cathedral and castle.

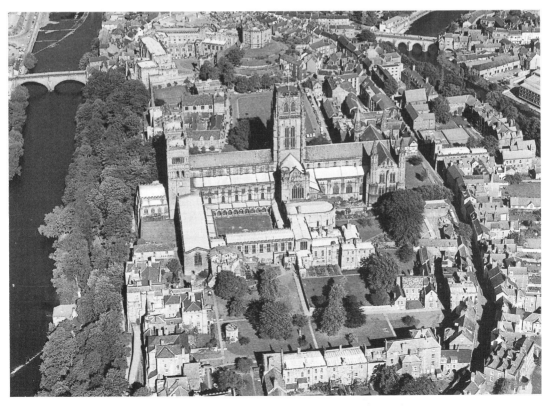

66. Spanish Battery, Tynemouth: Tudor artillery emplacement, re-used in modern period.

67. Lindisfarne Castle: Tudor castle guarding anchorage, subsequently converted into distinctive modern house.

families, or prince-bishops of Durham, but were erected by the English Crown. On the headland close to that on which Tynemouth Priory and Castle stand (see 2), lies the Spanish Battery (66). The original construction of this bastion guarding the little harbour near the Tyne entrance may date back to the reign of Henry VIII; its name is traditionally associated with its first garrison, a body of Spanish mercenary troops in that king's pay. Alterations and adaptations were made at various times in the 17th and 18th centuries, followed by the creation of artillery emplacements of the 19th and 20th centuries. Some of these are still visible in this photograph, though since this was taken a short-sighted decision has covered or removed them completely, thereby reducing an interesting and complex historical monument to an anonymous grassy mound. In early times there seems to have been a system of walls and further defences linking the battery to the main works of the castle, but little or nothing of these can now be made out.

Further up the Northumberland coast, an anchorage on Lindisfarne provided a stage on the English supply route to the border. About 1550 a small castle (67) was built to command this anchorage.[17] The recently dissolved priory provided an apt source of readily available stone, while the island itself provided lime for mortar. The castle continued in existence in the 17th century, when a report of 1639 listed in its lower battery

> 3 iron peeces and 2 of brasse, with carriadges and platformes in good order. On the higher was one brasse gun and two iron ones with all ammunition to them.

A small garrison remained until 1820, and thereafter the castle, in deteriorating condition, served as a coastguard station and then as a headquarters for the local Volunteer troops. In 1902 it was bought by Edward Hudson, owner of *Country Life*, who commissioned his friend Edwin Lutyens to restore the castle for him. The restoration provided a house of great character if no great historical authenticity.[16] The castle was given to the National Trust in 1944.

The continuing concern of the Tudor monarchy with the northern border, and the considerable sums expended in this area by that government, are most eloquently illustrated by the defences of Berwick (68) — the best early modern town defences in Great Britain. Queen Elizabeth I spent here a total of £128,648 5s. 9$\frac{1}{2}$d., making the Berwick defences the biggest single item of government expenditure during her long reign.[19] The old castle of Berwick was out of date by this time, and in the reign of Mary Tudor England's greatest expert in defensive works, Sir Richard Lee, was sent to make plans for equipping this key border town with defences which would take into account latest advances in artillery and siegecraft. Lee had recently been engaged in providing Portsmouth with stronger defences designed on the lines of the best continental examples. He came to Berwick in January 1558, and laid down the designs for a major programme. By 1561, 1,000 men were employed. A principal objective was to ensure that any hostile approach to the walls could be met by strongly emplaced artillery fire from at least two directions, and that no approach to the town was left uncovered by lanes of fire. The walls themselves, immensely strong, were some 20 feet high (not very different from the effective height both of Hadrian's Wall and many modern prisons). The

68. Berwick: Tudor defences around border stronghold.

projecting bastions remain the most striking feature and although some damage was done to these superb fortifications in the early 19th century, Berwick upon Tweed remains a marvellous example of a fortified town of the later 16th century. The area enclosed by the formidable new defensive perimeter was less extensive than the earlier urban area, and military necessity involved the demolition of buildings to give the defensive artillery a clear field of fire. If the Berwick fortifications reflect the last stages of major border warfare, the town's old bridge was one of the first fruits of the Union of the Crowns in 1603. It was built between 1610 and 1634 as an important new link within James I's new Kingdom of Great Britain. In this photograph the old bridge, with its 15 arches, lies to the left of the more sophisticated, if not conspicuously beautiful, bridge of 1925-8.

If in the 16th century border warfare still entailed a high level of military expenditure, with the union of the Crowns in 1603 a major change took place, which was speedily reflected in the archaeological record. At Chipchase Castle (69) in the North Tyne valley, this shift is well exemplified. At the back of the buildings in this photograph there is a recognisable tower house of late medieval type — a small castle in fact, with obvious military characteristics, probably dating from the mid-14th century. Lying in front of it, and largely replacing it as a residence, is the

69. Chipchase Castle: Jacobean mansion added to medieval castle.

70. Redesdale Iron Works: ruins of early iron works in Northumberland countryside.

most beautiful Jacobean house in the region. An E-shaped structure dating from 1621, Jacobean Chipchase shows that as early as the reign of James I a Northumberland landowner could contemplate living no longer in a castle but in a home and a distinctly stately home at that. The large projecting windows over the door are original, but the projecting side windows were a 19th-century addition. There were other alterations in the 1780s, but the most important archaeological significance of Chipchase is its indication of the arrival of relative peace on the Anglo-Scottish border by the early 17th century.

This inaugurated a quickening of the pace of social and economic change, an acceleration which was to continue to our own day. The development of a new regional economy may be introduced by a site which is not always immediately appreciated. Many travellers driving along the A68 a few miles north of the Roman temporary camp at Fourlaws (8) assume that they are passing the keep of a border castle when they pass a square stone structure at Ridsdale (70). It is in fact the engine house of the Redesdale Iron Works, a little enterprise founded in the mid-1830s to exploit the conjunction of local deposits of coal, ironstone and lime.[20] Coke-making and brick-making became associated activities, but the enterprise failed in the early 1860s; no doubt transport problems in this remote area provided part of the explanation. Equipment which was useful and portable was transferred to Armstrong's growing works at Elswick on Tyneside. This little site reminds us that the great upsurge of economic growth in the Victorian North East involved a complex pattern of events which allowed for many individual failures within a general pattern of success. In this photograph the two parallel buildings below the roofless engine house were the works office and the school built for the workers' children. The parallel earthworks towards the top of the photograph are the remains of coke ovens. The blast furnaces were placed in the hollows just above the engine house.

In the course of the 19th century the society and the economy of the region were transformed. This did not mean a wholesale transfer of power from the older ruling groups to new men. Everywhere in Britain the old aristocracy took some part in the building of the new industrial society, but their role was particularly prominent in this region. Many country mansions were built with funds largely derived from non-agricultural sources. Seaton Delaval Hall (71) may be the region's most beautiful house. It is an early illustration of the entrepreneurial spirit of many of the region's landowners.

Vanbrugh designed the mansion for the Delaval family and it was built in 1718-29. The income which enabled that landed family to maintain its aristocratic life style was not confined to an agricultural rent roll, but came to include coal mines, a harbour and an important glass works. Wynyard Park (72) provides an even clearer example. The original plan here meant grafting on to the late 18th-century house of the coal-owning Vane Tempest family a grandiose concept originally designed by Benjamin Dean Wyatt as a suitable palace for the Duke of Wellington. The house was built for the third Marquess of Londonderry, who had married the Vane Tempest heiress in 1819. The scheme was executed between 1822 and 1828, but a disastrous fire in 1841 resulted in an even more sumptuous partial reconstruction.

Most of the revenue applied to this palatial building was derived from coal (see also 78 and 79), for the Marquess was one of the greatest of the Durham coal-owners.

The aristocratic mansions of the region experienced a variety of fates in later years. Close House (73), in the Tyne valley near Wylam, is a fine mansion of 1779. This replaced an older house on the site, which had come into the hands of the Bewick family, successful Newcastle merchants, in the 17th century. During the 20th century the mansion saw a variety of occupants before eventually being purchased by Newcastle University during the great period of university expansion after the Second World War. The extensive grounds are mainly used as sports fields, but the university's observatory and other experimental installations are also situated here. Gibside (74) is another example of an aristocratic mansion derived from varied sources of income, though it is now only a pathetic ruin.

Gibside was originally an early 17th-century house built by the Blakiston family, but its great days came after Sir George Bowes moved here in 1725, having married a Blakiston heiress. Bowes was another great coal magnate, a leading member of the Grand Allies who dominated the coal trade for many years. He made some alterations to the house but also surrounded it with an extensive park ornamented with such features as a banqueting house, an orangery, a fine chapel and a column representing British Liberty (Bowes was one of the region's leading Whigs). The estate came into the hands of the Earls of Strathmore in 1767, after the 9th Earl's marriage to Sir George Bowes' daughter. The 10th Earl removed the hall's third storey in the early 19th century, and substituted the heavily crenellated parapet. Regular occupation of the house ended over a century ago, and the main building was gutted by fire in 1920. The chapel, the orangery and parts of the grounds have been restored in more recent years.

Although economic developments led to an increasing emphasis on other elements, the agriculture of the region was itself much affected by technological developments in the 19th century. It was not until the last decades of the 19th century that the rural population within the region began to decline. The best farms of the North East enjoyed a high reputation for skill and technical inventiveness, though the record was a mixed one, and examples of agricultural backwardness were not difficult to find. There are many examples of the well-designed planned 19th-century farms in both Northumberland and Durham, but one example must suffice here. Until a few years ago Woodhorn Farm (75) stood about a mile north east of Ashington. This was for many years the centre of activity of one of the most famous of Northumberland farmers, Jacob Wilson. He came to Woodhorn in 1855, and in ensuing years introduced a variety of up-to-date methods — in 1857 an improved reaping machine, in 1865 the second set of paired steam ploughing engines to be built. In 1866 he became agent for the Earl of Tankerville's Chillingham estate. His status in farming circles may be comprehended from the knighthood conferred on him in 1889 for services to agriculture, a rare distinction for one of his position in Victorian Britain. Although the buildings have now all disappeared, the photograph shows how the main farm block, with its attached stockyards, was designed as a whole, with a steam engine soon incorporated to provide power for threshing and other processes.

71. Seaton Delaval Hall: Vanbrugh masterpiece in south-east Northumberland.

72. Wynyard Park: early 19th-century mansion in south Durham built for 3rd Marquess of Londonderry.

73. Close House: 18th-century mansion in Tyne valley.

74. Gibside: ruin of mansion once owned by Sir George Bowes and then by Earls of Strathmore.

Not all of the industrial elements which went to make up the new regional economy were to enjoy sustained success throughout the 19th century. Not only did some individual enterprises like the Redesdale Iron Works fail; there were cases of whole industries which grew to considerable size, only to wither away when circumstances turned against them. Lead-mining is perhaps the best example of this. This sector has a long history within the region — the fort at Whitley Castle, near Alston, was probably situated there to supervise Roman lead mines. The industry continued in medieval times, began to expand rapidly in the 18th century and reached a peak in the third quarter of the 19th century, to decline rapidly

75. Woodhorn Farm: planned Victorian farm layout with steam engine near Ashington.

thereafter in the face of increased costs as more accessible lodes were worked out, and unbeatable competition from imports of cheaper foreign lead. In recent years the archaeological evidence for the 19th-century lead industry has received increased study. Killhope (76), for many years an abandoned ruin, has been transformed into a major example of industrial archaeology and a tourist attraction. The lead ore crushing mill here stands near the head of Weardale in an area abounding with remains of large scale mining. Lead workings ran into the hill within a few hundred yards of the site. Ore was brought out of the workings and dumped in an area marked by low parallel lines in the centre of this photograph;

these were the 'bouse-steads', bouse being the local term for untreated ore. The divisions here enabled the ore produced by different teams of miners to be kept separate for assessment of earnings. Reservoirs far up the hill to the right of the area shown here provided a flow of water running down an aqueduct feeding the large overshot water wheel which powered the machinery for crushing the district's unusually hard lead-bearing rock. This water supply was also used for washing the crushed ore. The Killhope mill was part of the Beaumont family's extensive lead interests, another example of aristocratic landowners with industrial concerns. The existing mill was built in the 1870s to replace an earlier crushing mill on the same site.

When the lead ore had been crushed and washed to remove some of its impurities, smelting was the next major stage. Northumberland and Durham possess impressive industrial monuments in the remains of the great flues which carried the fumes from the smelters. Some of these passages ran for literally miles, and in some cases long stretches survive. The flues had two main purposes. One was to carry the poisonous fumes to safer discharge points, the other was to provide a facility for recovering profitable deposits accumulated in the flues. Early examples might consist only of a very long tunnel culminating in a hill-top chimney; good examples of these simple designs exist in Durham at Rookhope and Stanhope, in Northumberland at Allendale Town and Langley. At Castleside (77), near Consett, the design is more sophisticated than the long, slightly inclined type often used. It occupies a smaller area within which the fumes passed along a series of channels slowly mounting the hillside above the smelting area, culminating in a short chimney or 'stalk' near the summit. The original name of the site was Healeyfield, and the Healeyfield company worked here from 1805 to 1913.

Despite examples of failure, North-East England's economic development during the 19th century was overall a remarkable success story. Nor is it a tale of merely local or regional interest. The short period 1850-1914 saw some of the most important of all historical changes, including a ten-fold increase in the scale of international trading. In this great age of coal, iron and steam, North-East England played a significant part. King Coal was the sovereign dominating this expansion, for coal was not only a vital factor in the region's trade with other parts of Britain and elsewhere but provided the attraction responsible for the development on or near the coalfield of a range of major coal-using industries.

In the first decade of the 19th century the region's coal output was about 4.5 million tons; by 1851 it was about 10.5 million, with an increase in employment from 12,000 to 40,000. This significant expansion appears small only in comparison with the gigantic leap in production which followed — 1861, 19.5 million, 1871, 39 million, 1901, 45 million, 1911, 56.5 million tons. Employment in coal mining grew from 40,000 in 1851 to 96,000 in 1881 and 216,000 in 1911. The coal from Northumberland and Durham made a vital contribution to the evolution of modern Britain and a wider world beyond; it was won at a high cost in death, injury and suffering. The remains of this great industrial interest, now in marked decline, are among the most precious elements in the region's archaeological heritage, for the collieries and the staiths, the waggonways and the pit villages, provided a vital

76. Killhope: ruins of water-powered lead ore crushing plant in west Durham.

77. Castleside: ruins of 19th-century lead-smelting site.

element in the world's energy supplies during a major period of historical transformation. If, in the Roman Empire, this peripheral region was of little value to the Mediterranean-based state, in the much larger British Empire of the Victorian period the Great Northern Coalfield was an important source of strength and wealth.

Just to the north of Seaham Harbour on the Durham coast lies the Vane Tempest Colliery (78). This pit was created in 1923-8 by the use of sophisticated sinking methods to replace the old Seaham pit, which was becoming inefficient as coal nearer to it was increasingly worked out. Vane Tempest now works undersea deposits, and was for many years complemented by Dawdon Colliery, sunk to the south of Seaham Harbour in 1899-1907. The Stewart Marquesses of Londonderry acquired the additional names of Vane Tempest by marriage to a Durham heiress in 1819, and subsequently developed a great coal enterprise of which these two collieries formed one important element. The Lambton Earls of Durham were another leading aristocratic family with major mining interests in County Durham.

At Seaham Harbour (79) the third Marquess of Londonderry built a coal-shipping harbour to which the coal from some of his collieries could be carried along his railway. The original small harbour begun in the 1820s — the lower right part of the harbour complex in this photograph — grew by the early 20th century into complex harbour installations owned by the Londonderry Coal Company. The size and complexity of the coal-loading staiths here (80) show clearly what the harbour's main business was. It was not only at Seaham Harbour that the expanding coalfield produced extensive facilities apart from the pits and the mining communities themselves. Similar developments took place on Tyneside. The Albert Edward Dock (81) was the second large dock on the river to be built by the Tyne Improvement Commission. The T. I. C. came into existence at mid-century, after a prolonged struggle between the town of Newcastle, whose ancient charters conferred a monopoly control over the whole Tyne harbour, and the other Tyneside communities championing the interests of port-users. The struggle provides an excellent example of the interaction of economic, social and political factors. Newcastle struggled hard for the retention of its profitable rights in the port, but when Gateshead, Tynemouth and South Shields obtained their own M.P.s and municipal institutions they were better equipped to mount a successful assault on the monopoly which hampered their interests.

Political pressure and subsequent legislation were indispensable here. Without the creation of the T. I. C. at mid-century, and the river improvements then set in motion, the economic and social history of modern Tyneside would have been very different. The Albert Edward Dock was built in the years around 1880, using the mouth of the Coble Dene as its focus. From the beginning, coal-shipping was a major part of its functions. There were other interests, equally allied to the development of the emerging industrial society. The large building to the right of the dock in this photograph was a grain warehouse (demolished with some difficulty in 1973), involved in the increased imports of food needed by the growing population of Tyneside. The complex railway system serving the dock can be appreciated here. The quays along the riverfront provided terminals for the

78.   Vane Tempest Colliery: colliery sunk in 1920s to replace older Seaham colliery.

79.   Seaham Harbour: coal-shipping harbour founded by 3rd Marquess of Londonderry.

80. Seaham Harbour Staiths: coal-shipping installations.

81. Albert Edward Dock: 19th-century dock built in mouth of Coble Dene on north bank of Tyne.

82. Dene Staith: ruin of coal-shipping installation in Albert Edward Dock.

83. Whitehill Point: 20th-century coal staith on north bank of Tyne, with traces of earlier staiths.

important sea links with Scandinavia. At the rear of the dock lie the mouldering ruins of the Dene Staith (82), the dock's main coal-shipping facility. Coal was first shipped over this timber structure on 21 August 1884 and it last worked on 1 January 1943.

At the end of the last century 18 separate coal staiths were working within a mile of the Albert Edward Dock. None of these now survive in operation, and the ending of coal shipments from the north bank of the Tyne marked the end of a long and important phase in the region's history. A little distance to the west of the Albert Edward Dock is Whitehill Point (83), where coal was shipped from 1855 until the 1970s. The last coal staith to work on the north bank of the Tyne was Berth A, shown on the left. With twin movable loading arms, this staith, erected in 1956, could ship a thousand tons an hour (a figure much exceeded by later designs). To the right can be seen the masonry stumps left from the older No. 1 and No. 2 staiths, still active in the inter-war years, while fainter traces remain of still earlier coal-shipping installations at Whitehill Point. Further up the Tyne, at Derwenthaugh (84), another staith shipped coal from collieries owned by the Consett Iron Company (see also 89), while a group of large tanks represents part of that company's associated trade in coal by-products. In 1948 Derwenthaugh was considered as a possible site for a new iron ore importing centre, but in the event this installation, ultimately short-lived, went to the Tyne Dock, further down-river.

The biggest single coal-shipping point in the coalfield was provided by the quartet of staiths in the Tyne Dock (85), to the west of South Shields. This dock opened in 1859 and until 1937, when it was taken over by the T. I. C., the installations belonged to the North Eastern Railway and its successor the L. N. E. R. The staiths were the central element in a complex dock; there were also bunkering facilities and installations for the import of timber and grain. In an aerial view the scale of the coal staiths can be appreciated, especially the 25 miles of railway sidings which lay behind the staiths themselves. The design allowed loaded and unloaded coal trains to be moved on and off the staiths by gravity; the impetus of loaded trucks running down to the staith pulled empty trucks back into the sidings. [17] The staiths here reached their maximum size in the early 1890s; four smaller staiths had preceded them on the same site. In 1888 nearly 5.5 million tons of coal were shipped here, but this was surpassed in the boom years just before 1914 and in the early 1920s when in one year 7.5 million tons were loaded. The staiths have been destroyed since this photograph was taken, and indeed only one was still working at that time. The railway sidings and the four massive stone arches which carried the coal trains over the Newcastle-South Shields road have also gone. Tyne Dock is now used for general cargo work, while a new coal-shipping installation and a modern bulk grain-shipping plant have been built by the port authority near Jarrow, a short distance to the west.

In some places the expansion of the coalfield and its dependent industries brought completely new communities into existence. The ancient borough of Hartlepool, originally chartered by medieval Bishops of Durham, observed with some distaste the growth of a younger rival at West Hartlepool (86) which soon outstripped the old town in size and wealth. Apart from coal-shipping staiths, one of

84. Derwenthaugh: coal staith and associated installations on south bank of Tyne west of Gateshead.

85. Tyne Dock: coal staiths in Tyne Dock on south bank of Tyne between South Shields and Jarrow.

this booming port's main concerns was the importation of the huge quantities of timber which the Durham mines consumed. Development here began in the 1830s and accelerated after the building of a railway link with Stockton in 1841, under the leadership of the energetic Ralph Ward Jackson. Although he fell from power in 1862 as a result of a company scandal, by that time the port was well established, with three deep-water docks, two grain docks, coal staiths, timber ponds and a variety of other installations which supported the growing population of the new town.

The industrial economy which developed during the Victorian period relied heavily upon a small group of connected industries, especially coal, iron and steel, shipbuilding and engineering. Partly because of the market for coal-carrying vessels, the North East became one of the world's foremost shipbuilding areas, although its role here was to decline markedly in the later 20th century. The Tyne saw the construction of some notable vessels, ranging from some of the last of the sailing ships for the East India Company through pioneering iron steamships and oil tankers to famous vessels of more recent years. The river Tyne is too narrow to provide an ideal context for the building of very large ships, but the Walker Naval Yard (87) exploited a bend in the river to provide adequate launching space. This yard was opened by Armstrong Whitworth during the last phase of the pre-1914 naval competition, in time to build in 1913 H. M. S. *Malaya*, a battleship presented to the Royal Navy by the Malayan rulers. The yard experienced hard times during the inter-war years. It closed in April 1928, then re-opened two years later to build the Furness Withy liner *Monarch of Bermuda*, which was completed in November 1931. Lack of further contracts then brought another closure, until in May 1934 the onset of re-armament provided contracts for the building of a group of warships which served in the Second World War, including the cruiser H. M. S. *Newcastle*, the battleship *King George V* and the aircraft carrier H. M. S. *Victorious*. After the Second World War a group of once famous liners were built here, including *Empress of England, Empress of Canada* and *Northern Star*. Later orders included car ferries, container ships and bulk carriers, but the yard was to be one of the victims of the contemporary recession in British shipbuilding. At Swan Hunter's main base at Wallsend (88), this photograph of August 1973 shows some of the enclosed working spaces which replaced the old open working areas of the shipyards. At a quayside which had seen the building of many famous ships of the past, the *World Unicorn*, a 250,000 ton tanker built for Ludlow Navigation Ltd., was completing after her launch in May. Although the Tyne had pioneered the building of oil tankers, the great increase in size of some of these vessels in the later 20th century posed problems for builders on the relatively narrow North-East rivers.

Coal-mining and shipbuilding were both connected to the manufacture of iron and steel. In County Durham, Consett developed very much as a company town dependent upon the Consett Iron Works (89), which built more than 2,000 houses here. Iron-working began here with the creation of the Derwent Iron Company in 1839-40, designed to exploit local reserves of iron ore and cheap coal. The local iron ore deposits proved disappointing and the cost of its extraction rose alarmingly. Nevertheless, the firm kept going until the bank which had been its

86. West Hartlepool: extensive docks and other port installations.

main prop failed in 1857. A new and stronger Consett Iron Company was formed in 1864, but despite its inland situation, the works depended on imported ore. [22] From 1872 onwards much of this came from Spain. At first the growing demand for rails for railway construction was a major market. When that showed signs of slowing down, the development of first iron and then steel shipbuilding provided an alternative massive market for ships' plates. The company also developed its own collieries and exploited the various by-products from both its coal and its iron interests. By about 1890 the works had switched from iron to steel, and Consett was producing about 170,000 tons of steel annually. For much of its history, good management enabled the works to survive despite the obvious disadvantages of its inland location. This photograph shows the works in its latter years, when it still employed about 7,500 and sustained the town of Consett. At centre right the range of low roofs contains the Plate Mill, completed in 1964. In front of this are the plants for manufacturing coke and oxygen. The complex mass in the centre includes the blast furnaces, and the long radiating arms represent various steel-making and rolling processes. Since this photograph was taken the works, unable to

87. Walker Naval Yard: shipyard established in early 20th century, closed in later 20th century.

88. Swan Hunters, Wallsend: large vessel approaching completion in a major shipyard on Tyne.

match the advantages of coastal sites better situated for ore imports, has been closed down (1980) and dismantled.

Industrial development brought with it significant social changes. The growth of the coalfield brought a proliferation of mining communities which played a

89.   Consett Iron Works: iron and later steel works of early Victorian foundation, closed in 1980 and demolished.

significant role in the region's culture. Ashington (90) is a community closely associated with Victorian mining developments. Large scale mining here began in the middle of the 19th century in an area previously occupied by a single farm. The rows of houses alongside the colliery installations here were built for its miners by the Ashington Coal Company during the third quarter of the 19th century. The quality of the housing here is better than workers had known in the past and superior to the slums existing in North-East towns at that time. Before the community was equipped with main drainage a narrow-gauge railway operated by the colliery company ran around the streets, using horse-drawn rolling stock to deliver concessionary coal to miners' houses and removing 'night soil' from the privies. The provision of sizeable gardens was a common feature of these pit villages. Ashington was built in two main sections; this earlier area was followed late in the century by the building of another large batch of colliery houses (91), known as the Hirst End of Ashington, associated with the opening of Woodhorn Colliery at the end of the 19th century. Although the two communities were very close to each other, and the collieries owned by the same company, their lives were so bound up with the two collieries that they largely went their separate ways socially for many years and traces of this separatism still remain today.

Boldon Colliery (92), between Newcastle and Sunderland, gives a good impression of the self-contained nature of most mining communities, if we ignore the encroaching tide of late 20th-century building nearby. Again the rows of colliery houses, of about 1879, lie close to the pit itself, with the colliery brickworks in the lighter patch of ground at centre left. The same impression is conveyed by a Northumberland example at Netherton (93, 94), about four miles west of Blyth. This is an area steeped in mining history, from the Glebe pit of the 1820s, sunk by George Stephenson and Michael Longridge; a steam engine was taken from this early colliery to work on the east end of the Stockton and Darlington Railway. The modern Netherton Colliery was still working in the early 1970s but its closure involved the end of the community. These 1969 photographs clearly reveal the layout of the village, though since they were taken it has been demolished. In the distant shot we are looking over the village towards the colliery, with the modern pithead baths lying to the left, close to the pit. The second photograph gives a closer view of the village itself. Most of the housing here was rebuilt by the colliery company about 1900. Again the large areas allotted as gardens stand out, and the self-contained nature of these scattered colliery communities is well illustrated here. Since these photographs were taken, both the colliery installations and the colliery houses have been destroyed. North Seaton (95, 96), near Ashington, provides a similar example. Here the colliery worked from 1861 to 1961. When the first photograph was taken the colliery had already been closed for some years, but most of the houses, ranging from the typical Victorian colliery square' in the foreground to distant semi-detached 20th-century houses at the far end, were still occupied. Subsequently, most of the residents were moved to a new (and more highly rented) North Seaton estate attached to nearby Ashington. The second photograph shows the fate of the village in subsequent years, only the modern housing at the east end surviving. Many of our colliery villages have now shared this fate, but they should not be forgotten, for they played a key role in what may be seen as the most important phase in the region's long history.

The growth of the region's modern towns provides in itself a complex story, and an individual centre could display contrasting traits. At Newcastle, in the valley of the Ouse Burn (97) to the east of the old town, from the 18th century and throughout the 19th century there developed a largely unplanned and confused mixture of industrial enterprises — glassworks, chemical works, a flax mill, potteries, engineering works — together with odd patches of housing with some shops and public houses. On the other hand, the early years of Victoria's reign saw a unique central area development, which provides the modern city with its finest

90. Ashington: mid-19th-century colliery and associated housing.

91. Ashington, Hirst End: late Victorian colliery housing.

92. Boldon Colliery: Durham mining village, *c*.1879.

93. Netherton: distant view of colliery and mining community.

94. Netherton: closer view of colliery housing, mainly re-built *c*.1900.

95. North Seaton: mid-Victorian and later colliery village near Ashington.

96. North Seaton: demolition of Victorian colliery village.

architectural inheritance. [23] The conjunction of a property developer, Richard Grainger, a group of local architects of whom John Dobson is the best known, and an able and influential Town Clerk, John Clayton, enabled a substantial area of the town to be developed (98, 99). The first photograph shows the new streets radiating from the Grey Monument at centre right. The second photograph gives a closer view of the new enclosed market complex, the Grainger Market, which lay at the heart of the scheme. On the right, near the top of the new Grey Street, can be picked out the porticoed front of the Theatre Royal and the neighbouring building originally erected as the headquarters of the leading local bank which helped to shore up iron-working at Consett in early Victorian years.

The unforeseen and unforeseeable scale of economic change during the 19th century posed serious problems for a society which possessed central and local government of only limited extent and quality. The towns of North-East England came to possess an unenviable position in the upper reaches of the well-known

97.   Newcastle, Ouseburn: industrial suburb to east of old town centre.

98. Central Newcastle: area of major redevelopment in early Victorian years.

99. Grainger Market, Newcastle: closer view of part of the early Victorian redevelopment.

Victorian tables of social problems. These problems appeared more telling in the rapidly growing towns, but they were not simply an urban problem. For example, the overcrowding figures from these towns for the years around 1900 are matched not only by the scattered mining communities but also by rural north Northumberland. [24] However, it was in the towns that concentration brought the worst conditions. At some remove in time, a new housing stock was created which began to catch up with the rapidly increasing population. Rows of new terrace housing were built, much of it in the form of the regionally distinctive 'Tyneside terrace flat'. At South Shields (100) the town had grown fast, with shipyards, chemical works, glass works and collieries all expanding. This photograph shows a large area of this late Victorian housing only a short distance from the Roman fort and the Baring Street school (4). A similar development lies in what were then the western fringes of Newcastle (101, 102, 103). The old town centre and the early Victorian new town lay out of sight above the area covered in the first two photographs. This block of housing, of a markedly different character from any earlier phase of the town's long history, provided part of the northern section of a thick belt of terrace housing, spreading from the riverside area to the west of the town centre, where the growth of the engineering and armaments industries was producing an ever-increasing housing demand. The third photograph shows part of the similar area at the southern end of the development, close to the Tyne and the massive industrial enterprises along its north bank.

The kind of urban society which was now emerging required services of many different kinds on an unprecedented scale. Literacy was more urgently required than at any earlier period and public involvement in the provision of schooling soon expanded. At North Shields the Western Board School (104) was one of three new schools planned in 1871 by the newly created Tynemouth School Board (see also 4). The main E-shaped building was designed for 582 children, with 284 infants in the adjacent infants' school. The 20th century saw the continuation of expansion in state-financed education. A contrast in architectural conceptions is shown in another part of North Shields (105), where the Tynemouth Municipal High School of 1904 on the left, a local grammar school created under the 1902 Education Act, was replaced by the Tynemouth Sixth Form College (seen here to the right of the older school), opened in September 1972 as part of the later 20th-century's vision of comprehensive education.

The region's resources for higher education also saw major developments. The centre of the next photograph is occupied by the crowded buildings of the University of Newcastle upon Tyne (106). To the left lie the buildings of the university's teaching hospital, the Royal Victoria Infirmary, which developed from an 18th-century charitable foundation into one of Britain's great modern medical centres. To the right, between the university and Newcastle Polytechnic's main campus, lies Newcastle's modern Civic Centre, with its circular Council Chamber. This municipal administrative headquarters illustrates the increased importance of local government in modern society, while its architectural scale reflects local government's complete awareness of its own importance. The growth in student numbers in recent years has had significant social implications. In Newcastle, the university and the polytechnic are now among the city's principal employers, and

100.   South Shields: high density terrace housing of late Victorian period.

101.   Newcastle: high density terrace housing to north west of old town centre.

102.   Newcastle: another view of terrace housing to north west of old town centre.

103.   Newcastle: high density terrace housing near Tyne to west of old town centre.

104. North Shields: mid-Victorian board schools.

105. North Shields: early 20th-century municipal grammar school and later 20th-century sixth form college.

106. Newcastle University: closely packed buildings on restricted central site.

107. Castle Leazes Halls:
university halls of residence
close to university site.

108. Newcastle: Keelmen's Hospital and Industrial Dwellings, preserved as accommodation for polytechnic students.

109. St Aidan's College, University of Durham.

the thousands of students enrolled in higher education bring useful spending power. Again the contemporary environment provides archaeological evidence of these developments. Close to the university, a group of modern halls of residence at Castle Leazes (107), if not notably beautiful, has done much to solve the housing problems associated with the university's expansion.

Along City Road, Newcastle (108), the increase in student numbers at the city's polytechnic has had interesting consequences for two of the city's historic buildings. The square courtyard building at lower centre is one of Newcastle's most important monuments, the Keelmen's Hospital of 1701. The keelmen manned the coal-carrying barges of the North East's rivers, the keels, before river improvements enabled large colliers to load directly anywhere in the lower Tyne. They formed a distinctive group in local society for many years. 'Hospital' here is used in its older sense of almshouses, and the Keelmen's Hospital provided accommodation for old keelmen and their dependents. It was originally financed by a levy on coal shipped by keel and by small regular payments by the keelmen. Its construction and administration were provided for in a special Act of Parliament obtained in 1699. Newcastle Corporation took over the administration of the building in 1872, but by the mid-20th century it had been allowed to deteriorate, though a restoration programme was then put in hand.

The long building immediately above the Keelmen's Hospital in this north-facing photograph is the Industrial Dwellings of 1870-9. [25] This large block of flats is the best example within the region of the kind of philanthropic housing project of which the Peabody Buildings in London are the best known. Headed by the shipowner John Hall, a group of leading Tynesiders clubbed together to provide the capital to build a block of housing for workers, accepting that their return from the rents paid, though real, would be lower than other forms of available investment — '5% philanthropy', as it was often called. Extensions to the original scheme were added in 1872 and 1878. Again the building had become run down by the mid-20th century. The preservation of such buildings is often dependent on a new use being found for them. Both the Keelmen's Hospital and the Industrial Dwellings have now been rehabilitated as accommodation for polytechnic students, with the added advantage of bringing a substantial number of new residents into an older area of the city which had been largely denuded of residents in previous years.

The region's older university, Durham, was created in the 1830s and remained very small for many years. The injection of public funds into higher education has involved more rapid growth in recent decades but, unlike most provincial universities, Durham has clung to the collegiate system. Since the Second World War, a group of new college buildings has been built. St Aidan's College (109) was designed in the 1960s by Sir Basil Spence. The college has developed from a group of women 'Home Students' added to the university in 1895, and forms part of a group of new college buildings in the city's western outskirts but within easy reach of the old centre. The modern extent of publicly financed facilities for higher education within the region would have astonished earlier generations.

The new industrial society brought increased income and increased leisure to the region's inhabitants and this has been exemplified in the development of extensive and varied recreational facilities. For generations the main Newcastle race meeting had been held annually on the Town Moor, but in 1881 a new race course was built at Gosforth. The race meeting on the Town Moor was replaced by an annual Temperance Festival which developed into one of the country's greatest fun fairs. The 1972 Town Moor Fair (110) was much smaller than its inter-war predecessors, largely because of the recent development of extended opportunities and more sophisticated tastes in holiday-making. The concept of overseas holidays had not spread far in North-East England before 1939, and the Race Week fair on the Town Moor, with the children off school and the father perhaps on holiday too, was often the standard family holiday outing.

Welcoming the Northumberland miners to their annual Picnic (equivalent to the Durham Miners' Gala) in 1910, the Mayor of Tynemouth expressed his pleasure that the pitmen had chosen to come to Tynemouth and not 'like the giddy folk, gone to Whitley Bay'. [26] Despite this not entirely disinterested comment, the rise of Whitley Bay as a local seaside resort was also part of the region's modern social history. Similar developments took place near the Wearside and Teesside industrial concentrations, in such places as Roker and Seaburn, Redcar and Saltburn. In part, Whitley Bay grew as a dormitory for Newcastle after the railway link was established in the mid-19th century, but the beaches and the added seaside leisure attractions also largely contributed to the town's growth. Behind the white dome of the Empress Ballroom at top centre, the amusement park known as The Spanish City (111) grew up; by the 1920s it possessed a Water Chute, Figure Eight Railway, Social Whirl, Joy Wheel, Flying Airships, Hall of Laughter, Maze, Rainbow Wheel and a host of sideshows.

The continued growth of the region's urban areas has been a marked feature of the present century, and some of the housing involved has a particular historical interest. Between Tynemouth and Whitley Bay, the 1930s brought the construction of a great mass of small semi-detached houses, of which a large area at Cullercoats (112) is shown here. National housing legislation was partly responsible for the decline in regionally distinct housing types like the Tyneside terrace flat, and these inter-war houses at Cullercoats could be in any part of Britain. They have an additional historical interest. Such houses were built in thousands, in the North East as elsewhere, and provide eloquent archaeological evidence that the region's social experience in the inter-war years was distinctly mixed rather than universally a story of depression and suffering. The problems facing the region's old staple industries of coal, iron and steel, shipbuilding and engineering, produced large scale unemployment and deprivation, but the majority of the region's population enjoyed an improving standard of living in these years. New houses like these are part of that story.

Since the Second World War, urban growth has continued; indeed, these very modern decades, and not the Victorian age, provide the classical period of the swallowing up of rural areas by urban expansion. As in earlier periods, the housing of the later 20th century has been of varied character. Some of it is embodied in the new towns which have been created as deliberate acts of policy by either central or local government agencies. Most of these schemes were sanctioned in the 1960s, when post-war confidence in official planning remained high. Killingworth New Town was designed to establish a new community of some 20,000 people to relieve

110. Newcastle Town Moor Fair, 1972.

111. Spanish City fun fair, Whitley Bay.

112.   Cullercoats: large block of inter-war housing.

housing pressures elsewhere. Designs were mixed, and the results have been equally mixed. Much of the housing here has survived, but the 'deck access' high-rise housing area known as 'The Citadel' or the Killingworth Towers (113) has been something of a planning disaster. Designed to provide 740 homes, the tower blocks, with their connecting walkways, were built in 1968, and won an important design award the next year. During the 1970s, their troubles mounted, and by August 1985, 418 of the 740 housing units were empty. The blocks had an exceptionally bad crime record and were locally known as 'Colditz'. Recriminations between designers and council managers were perhaps to be expected, the former blaming the disaster on a council housing policy which produced a concentration of 'problem tenants', the latter speaking of 'design inadequacies' as at least partly responsible. [27] As late as May 1985, the local council was putting on a brave face, and talking of 'special steps' to rehabilitate the blocks, but only a few months later the council reluctantly decided to abandon the struggle. The blocks were demolished early in 1988 at a cost of *c*. £2 million.

A second view of Killingworth New Town (114) illustrates another feature of the increasingly urbanised and sophisticated modern society, the extraordinary growth in the scale and complexity of retail and distributive services which are now required and available. In the town centre the largest flat-roofed building provided one of the early large shopping facilities situated outside the major town centres. This Woolco centre was intended to attract customers not only from the new town's 20,000 population but also from a much wider area. Greater real incomes and a more mobile population, with car owning much more common, brought changes in shopping habits. Developments such as Newcastle's Eldon Square shopping precinct and Gateshead's Metro Centre are later examples of the extended retail facilities which ought to be seen as a major historical phenomenon.

Other new towns of the region, while often embracing non-traditional architectural concepts, have avoided disasters such as Killingworth's central Citadel housing. In County Durham, 55,000 acres were set aside for the creation of Washington New Town (115, 116) in 1964, in an area containing many closed collieries. Here the plan aimed at a partly decentralised community, with an attempt to provide social coherence in the form of 'villages', each of about 4,500 population. The housing may not be particularly beautiful, but at least it has survived in use. In addition to the planned creation of new communities, housing in the region's older towns has seen considerable sprawl into previously open country in the years since 1945. Examples include an area of mixed types of modern housing in part of Gateshead's southern expansion (117), and housing built by Sunderland Corporation at Doxford Park (118) in the later 1960s.

The task of replacing the employment lost by the staple industries of the region in the inter-war years has proved a difficult one, but the extent of public investment in such efforts has grown considerably. An early example was the Team Valley Trading Estate (119). In August 1935 the government's Commissioner for Special Areas reported that he had been converted to 'the novel and unorthodox proposal of establishing trading estates financed out of Exchequer Funds'. [28] One of the first fruits of this gingerly introduced exercise in intervention was the North East Trading EstatesLtd. , a company formed in May 1936 to acquire and prepare trading estates which could encourage new enterprises. The Team Valley site, their first major effort, covered 700 acres and by May 1939 was providing 2,520 jobs, though relatively few of these were the jobs for skilled adult men which the area mainly needed. Under the pressure of wartime needs, employment here leaped to 15,000. There was some decline after 1945, but by 1952 the estate was again providing 12,000 jobs; by 1970 Team Valley held 106 firms with a total of 15,000 jobs. Local authorities sought to imitate such initiatives both before and after the war. Tynemouth Corporation took up the task again after 1945 and one of its early successes resulted in the attraction of the Formica firm (120), with its 600 jobs, to the council's West Chirton Trading Estate in 1947. The Alcan aluminium smelter at Lynemouth (121) is an example of an enterprise attracted to the region by direct intervention of the central government. A local colliery provides about a million tons of coal annually for the small power station at left centre, which in turn powers the electrical smelting plant at centre right. The building of this complex, at a capital cost of £65 million, was heavily subsidised in order to bring employment and income to a declining mining area. The scheme provides about a thousand jobs,

113.   Killingworth New Town: tower blocks which formed unsuccessful housing project of 1960s.

114.   Killingworth New Town: new town centre, including Woolco supermarket.

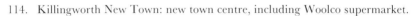

115. Washington New Town: modern housing forming individual community of limited size as part of new town.

116. Washington New Town: closer view of this housing project.

117. Gateshead: later 20th-century expansion of housing to south of older town.

118. Gateshead: another block of modern housing, part of Gateshead's southern extension in recent decades.

and two similar installations were also subsidised in Wales and the Scottish Highlands in the 1960s.

Some areas of the region's economy have flourished independently. The chemical industry has a long history within the region. During the 19th century Tyneside was a major centre, but in the late 19th and early 20th centuries the centre moved away to Teesside, where it has continued. During the First World War a small plant was established at Billingham (122) and the firm of Brunner Mond & Co. continued to develop it after 1918. In 1923 ammonia, in 1927 fertilisers and in 1928 methanol, joined the list of products. Later still, synthetic fibres were added to the list and Billingham has continued as one of the major installations of Imperial Chemical Industries. During the 1960s more than £33 million was spent in modernising the company's Teesside plants. About 15,000 people are employed here.

Economic development within the region has depended heavily upon the availability of good transport networks. River and sea carriage provided one of the fundamental advantages which led to the area's industrial growth, but rail and road developments have been important too. The bridges between Newcastle and Gateshead (123, 124) provide another example of the dependence of the modern world on more sophisticated channels of communication. In the first photograph a trio of bridges appears. The central low-lying Swing Bridge lies on the site of the medieval and early modern bridges, and indeed on the site of the Roman bridge which gave Newcastle its first known name of *Pons Aelius* — the bridge of Hadrian. The Swing Bridge was completed in 1876, replacing a low-level bridge of 1779 with multiple arches which prevented any sizeable vessels from passing up-river. Until the later 20th century the swinging centre of the later bridge was operated wholly by the hydraulic machinery installed by Armstrong when the bridge was built; now electricity is the prime mover, though much of the original machinery is still employed. This opening of a larger passageway made it possible for large ships to proceed up-river, and this allowed the massive development of Armstrong's Elswick works, especially in shipbuilding, though by the early 20th century the width of the passage through the bridge could already provide an uncomfortable limitation on ship design up-river. In the early years of this century the Swing Bridge would open scores of times each day; with very little traffic proceeding up-river, this facility is now only infrequently used.

To the left of the Swing Bridge lies the High Level Bridge of 1845-9; both a rail and a road bridge, it represents the united design talents of the engineer Robert Stephenson and the architect John Dobson. The 10,000 tons of iron needed were provided from local iron works. As well as providing a high-level crossing linking the growing towns of Newcastle and Gateshead, the bridge provided a crucial link in the main north-south railway connection between London and Edinburgh. To the right of the Swing Bridge is the Tyne Bridge of 1925-8; this provided Newcastle and Gateshead with a more direct north-south road link along a new axis, and illustrated the 20th-century revival in road transport. Curving away from the north end of the two high-level bridges is a line of railway running off to the east to connect Newcastle with communities along the Tyne and in other nearby areas. This

119. Team Valley Trading Estate: early example of 20th-century regional policy.

120. North Shields: Formica factory, Coast Road.

121. Lynemouth, Alcan Smelter: new industry brought to declining mining area.

122. Billingham: part of major I.C.I. chemical installations near mouth of Tees.

123. Tyne Bridges.

124. Tyne Bridges.

development began with the Newcastle and North Shields Railway of 1839, and as the suburban rail network expanded it exercised an important influence on the growth of nearby towns and villages.

In the second photograph, looking from the west, we see nearly all of the Tyne bridges here. There are two more westerly additions to the trio already mentioned. The nearer one is the 'old' Redheugh Bridge, in fact a 1901 replacement of an 1871 original; the decision to replace the 1871 design may have owed something to its use of gas and water mains as important load-bearing structures. The building of the 19th-century Redheugh Bridge provides a good example of how such enterprises could have important social consequences. The bridge linked the expanding western suburbs of Newcastle and Gateshead, enabling many workers living in the masses of terrace housing in west Gateshead to cross the river to work in Armstrong's Elswick works and similar enterprises. Among other consequences this

125.   Carrville intersection: example of modern road network, overlying earlier transport systems.

meant that Gateshead must carry any social problems arising in such housing areas, while the rate income from the employing works went to the local authority in Newcastle. This was one factor in ensuring that Newcastle was better equipped to cope with social problems than its poorer sister town, at a time when central government subsidies to local official activity remained meagre. Since this photograph was taken, this bridge has once again (1981) been replaced by a more modern and wider version. A little further down-river lies the King Edward VII railway bridge, opened in 1906 for the North Eastern Railway. This, with the High Level Bridge to the east, provides Newcastle's fine Central Station (which lies just out of view to the left) with good approaches over the river at either end. One modern bridge is missing in this view of 1971. The development of suburban transport, with its implications for places of residence and employment, has continued during the later 20th century. The modern Tyneside rapid transit system, the Metro, was, in 1980, provided with its own bridge, erected between the High Level and the King Edward VII bridges.

In the 20th century, the internal combustion engine has restored to road transport much of its earlier primacy in internal communications. At Carrville (125) in County Durham, there is a typical example of a modern road intersection as the A1(M) passes under the Sunderland-Durham A690 road. The 34 miles of the Durham Motorway were built in the later 1960s, overcoming geological problems which earlier generations would have found difficult. Older communications have also left their traces here. From the railway viaduct towards top left a railway of 1867 linked the old main line of the North Eastern Railway with the Durham and Bishop Auckland Railway. From centre right an older line can still be picked out to the right of the motorway intersection. This was part of the Newcastle and Darlington Junction Railway of 1844. The apparently abrupt end to this line is explained by the fact that the building of the road intersection destroyed part of the remaining traces, while to the left the line was covered by the modern road running towards Durham.

Improved communications, often involving major schemes of engineering and construction and requiring some form of political action to authorise their construction, may usefully introduce another key feature of the region's modern society. At Sunderland, the Ryhope water pumping station (126) presents an interesting technical example of industrial archaeology, but its historical significance goes deeper than that. It is a good example of the public utilities which play an important role in the modern world. [29] This station was built for the Sunderland and South Shields Water Company and began working in 1868; it stopped pumping on 1 July 1969. From the late 18th century onwards there had been attempts to provide this area of east Durham with a better water supply, but it was not until this company began its work that anything effective was done. The Ryhope installations cost £58,416 and were designed by Thomas Hawksley, a leading expert in this specialised field of engineering. The engines were supplied by the Tyneside engineering form of Hawthorns. Both the engines themselves and the buildings of the pumping station were embellished with decorative features aimed at producing an enhancement of the local environment.

The arrival of a decent water supply for washing, cooking and drinking was an undoubted boon to the local communities, but it exemplified a change in social organisation which is of crucial importance in modern society even if it is not always fully appreciated. Interdependence between people has been a historical norm since earliest times, but the prevailing pattern over most of history has been a kind of intimate interdependence between families or neighbours, between people who

126.   Ryhope Pumping Station: steam-powered water pumping station in outskirts of Sunderland.

127.   Blyth Power Station: coal-fired generating station on Northumberland coast north of Blyth.

lived and worked together, who knew each other. In the more sophisticated industrialised and urbanised societies of the modern world this aspect of society has become much more complex. The inhabitants of South Shields, Sunderland and neighbouring communities acquired an undoubted bonus with the availability of a reliable water supply, but with it came a new kind of dependence upon the handful of specialised workmen who kept the steam engines at Ryhope and the sister stations working. In Northumberland a similar example is provided at Blyth Power Station (127), essentially a post-Second World War development. Blyth developed as a coal-shipping port and appropriately this is a coal-fired power station. We all depend upon the continuous flow into the national grid of electricity from this and similar power stations. That flow of current depends upon the work of specialised power station workers who do not know the overwhelming majority of those whom they supply with a vital service. They themselves are utterly dependent upon other people whom they do not know to supply them with food, clothing, education, entertainment, transport and a host of the other services which we all take for granted.

At South Shields the General Hospital (128) offers a parallel. Originally built in 1879-80 as the workhouse of the South Shields Poor Law Union, the main blocks of buildings on either side were essentially residential, and by 1900 the central group, slightly set back, was already a sizeable hospital for the town's poorer inhabitants.

128. South Shields General Hospital: mid-Victorian workhouse developed into modern hospital.

129. Smith's Dock, North Shields: group of varied vessels in Tyneside yard, 1973.

Since then the whole site has evolved into a major hospital, where again doctors, nurses and administrators provide vital services to a catchment area which far outstrips the limits of an individual's acquaintance. Within a handful of generations, the development of the sophisticated agencies of local and central government, including their welfare responsibilities, is yet another facet of the radically changing patterns of interdependence within a society like ours.

New patterns of interdependence are not confined to changes within the regional or national community, as can be illustrated in our last photograph, which shows a group of ships in Smith's Dock, North Shields (129) in August 1973. Three of them are of particular interest. To the right lay a Cunarder built on the Clyde in the 1950s, one of a pair then awaiting conversion and transfer to the Russian merchant navy as cruise ships in the Black Sea. The vessel with open holds moored at the quayside had just brought into the Tyne a cargo of iron ore for Consett from the Newfoundland ore field which was extensively exploited from the 1960s. She was Sunderland-built, German-owned and Panama-registered. The slab-sided' vessel in the dry dock built in 1954 began life at Belfast in 1960 as the 20,000-ton Royal Mail liner *Aragon*. In 1969 she made the last Royal Mail run to South America, on a route which had seen 118 years of continuous service. She was then transferred to Shaw Savill and employed on that line's South Africa-Australia-New Zealand run as the *Aranda*. In 1971 she was bought by the Norwegian shipowner Leif Heogh, who had her converted in a Jugoslav yard to a mass car carrier. Fitted with 10 decks, she was then chartered alternately to Volkswagen to ship cars to America and to Nissan to bring cars from Japan to Britain. When this photograph was taken she had just entered the dock for survey and repair after delivering 3,472 Japanese vehicles to Teesside.

A thread of historical continuity links our own world to the first human visitors to this region about 10,000 years ago. The changing patterns of human interdependence have been one of the clearest demonstrations that recent generations have been capable of giving the long story of the evolution of human society a distinctive twist of their own.

Notes

1.   G. Jobey, 'Excavation at Tynemouth Priory and Castle', *Archaeologia Aeliana*, 4th Ser., XLV, 1967, pp. 33-104.

2.   R. J. Cramp, 'Excavations at the Saxon Monastic sites of Wearmouth and Jarrow, Co. Durham ...', *Medieval Archaeology*, XIII, 1969, pp. 21-66.

3.   D. J. Breeze, 'Excavations at the Roman Fort at Carrawburgh, 1967-9', *Archaeologia Aeliana*, 4th. Ser. L, 1972, pp. 81-144.

4.   I. A. Richmond, J. P. Gillam and E. B. Birley, 'The Temple of Mithras at Carrawburgh', *Archaeologia Aeliana*, 4th Ser., XXIX, 1951, pp. 1-92.For another Mithraic temple on the Wall, J. P. Gillam, I. MacIvor and E. B. Birley, 'The Temple of Mithras at Rudchester', *Archaeologia Aeliana*, 4th Ser., XXXII, 1954, pp. 176-219.

5.   G. Jobey, 'Hill Forts and Settlements in Northumberland', *Archaeologia Aeliana*, 4th Ser., XLIII, 1965, pp. 45-7.

6.   G. Jobey *et al.*, 'Excavations on palisaded settlements and cairnfields at Alnham, Northumberland', *Archaeologia Aeliana*, 4th Ser., XLIV, 1966, pp. 5-48.

7.   It is not possible to go into a detailed discussion of this complex matter here.The story of the successful exploitation of the limited evidence available can best be followed by reading the successive studies by Professor G. Jobey published in the 4th and 5th Series of *Archaeologia Aeliana*.

8.   The story can be followed in N. McCord and G. Jobey, 'Notes on Air Reconnaissance in Northumberland Durham: I.Tyne to Wansbeck, Northumberland', *Archaeologia Aeliana*, 4th Ser., XLVI, 1968, pp. 53-4; G. Jobey, 'A Native Settlement at Hartburn and the Devil's Causeway, Northumberland (1971)', *Archaeologia Aeliana*, 5th Ser., I, 1973, pp. 11-53; K. Greene, 'Apperley Dene Roman Fortlet: a re-examination, 1974-5', *Archaeologia Aeliana*, 5th Ser., VI, 1978, pp. 29-60.

9.   G. Jobey, 'An iron age settlement and homestead at Burradon, Northumberland', *Archaeologia Aeliana*, 4th Ser., XLVIII, 1970, pp. 51-95.

10.   E. A. Fisher, *Anglo-Saxon Towers*, Newton Abbot, 1969, pp. 49-50, 67. R. J. Cramp, 'Excavations at the Saxon Monastic Sites of Wearmouth and Jarrow, Co. Durham ...', *Medieval Archaeology*, XIII, 1969, pp. 21-66.

11.   B. Hope Taylor, *Yeavering: an Anglo-British centre of early Northumbria*, D.O.E., Archaeological Reports No. 7, 1977.

12.   T. Gates and C. O'Brien, 'Cropmarks at Milfield and New Bewick and the Recognition of Grubenhauser in Northumberland', *Archaeologia Aeliana*, 5th Ser., XVI, 1988, pp. 1-9.

13.   G. W. S. Barrow, 'The Anglo-Scottish Border', *Northern History*, I, 1966, pp. 21-42.G. W. S. Barrow, 'Northern English Society in the twelfth and thirteenth centuries', *Northern History*, IV, 1969, pp. 1-28. C. M. Fraser and K. Emsley, 'Law and Society in Northumberland and Durham, 1290-1350', *Archaeologia Aeliana*, 4th Ser., XLVII, 1969, pp. 47-70.

14.   W. Douglas Simpson, 'Dunstanburgh Castle', *Archaeologia Aeliana*, 4th Ser., XVI, 1939, pp. 1-28. W. Douglas Simpson, 'Further Notes on Dunstanburgh Castle', *Archaeologia Aeliana*, 4th Ser., XXVI, 1949, pp. 1-28.

15.   G. Jobey, 'Excavations at Tynemouth Priory and Castle', *Archaeologia Aeliana*, 4th Ser., XLV, 1967, pp. 33-104.

16.   B. W. Beckingsale, 'The Characteristics of the Tudor North', *Northern History*, IV, 1969, pp. 67-83.

17. *The History of the King's Works*, Vol. IV, 1485-1660, Part II, H.M.S.O. 1982, pp. 674-9.
18. C. Hussey, *The Life of Sir Edwin Lutyens*, 1950, pp. 106-7.
19. *The History of the King's Works*, op. cit., pp. 613-664.For the old Berwick bridge, ibid., pp. 769-78. I. MacIvor, *The Fortifications of Berwick-upon-Tweed*, H.M.S.O., 1972 (2nd. ed.).
20. R. F. Tylecote, 'Recent Research on nineteenth century Northumbrian blast furnace sites', *Industrial Archaeology*, 8, 1971, pp. 341-359.
21. T. E. Harrison, *On the Tyne Docks at South Shields: and the mode adopted for shipping coals*, 1860.
22. For a recent study of the history of Consett Iron Works, K. Warren, *Consett Iron 1840 to 1980: A Study in Industrial Location*, Oxford, 1990.
23. L. Wilkes and G. Dodds, *Tyneside Classical, the Newcastle of Grainger, Dobson and Clayton*, 1964.
24. N. McCord and D. J. Rowe, 'Industrialisation and Urban Growth in North East England', *International Review of Social History*, XXII, 1977. Part I, pp. 30-64.
25. W. Hayward, *James Hall of Tynemouth*, 1896, Vol. I, pp. 326-45.
26. I owe this information to Mr. Bill Purdue.
27. Killingworth West Moor Local Plan, North Tyneside Council, May 1985.
28. For a full study of this development, H. Loebl, *Government Factories and the Origins of British Regional Policy, 1934-1948*, 1988.
29. S. M. Linsley, *Ryhope Pumping Station*, Ryhope Engines Trust, 1973.

Index